OXFORD SHAKESPEARE STUDIES

*

MODERNIZING SHAKESPEARE'S SPELLING

WITH

THREE STUDIES IN THE TEXT OF *HENRY V*

Modernizing Shakespeare's Spelling

STANLEY WELLS

with

Three Studies in the Text of *Henry V*

GARY TAYLOR

OXFORD

AT THE CLARENDON PRESS

1979

Oxford University Press, Walton Street, Oxford OX2 6DP

OXFORD LONDON GLASGOW
NEW YORK TORONTO MELBOURNE WELLINGTON
KUALA LUMPUR SINGAPORE HONG KONG TOKYO
DELHI BOMBAY CALCUTTA MADRAS KARACHI
NAIROBI DAR ES SALAAM CAPE TOWN ,

Published in the United States by
Oxford University Press, New York

British Library Cataloguing in Publication Data

Wells, Stanley, *b. 1930*
    Modernizing Shakespeare's spelling
    1. Shakespeare, William—Language
    2. English language—Early modern, 1500–1700
      —Orthography and spelling
    3. Editing
    I. Title   II. Taylor, Gary
    822.3´3 PR3072 79-40664 ✓
    ISBN 0-19-812913-0

Printed in Great Britain
at the University Press, Oxford
by Eric Buckley
Printer to the University

PREFACE

In January 1978 Oxford University Press established a Shakespeare department with the primary aim of preparing new editions of Shakespeare's works. Almost fifty years before, R. B. McKerrow had embarked upon a related task, intending his edition to be among those which 'attempt to present Shakespeare's work as nearly in the form in which he left it as the evidence which we have permits, clearing it indeed as far as possible of the numerous errors with which the ignorance and carelessness of copyists and printers have disfigured it, but without superfluous comment or any attempt to improve upon the text as the author left it.' His 'main purpose' was to have been 'the establishment of the text', and he intended to give 'all available apparatus' to this end. As a preliminary to publication, and while working in detail on the texts of 'some ten plays', he wrote the *Prolegomena for the Oxford Shakespeare*, published in 1939. It has become a classic of textual criticism.

McKerrow died in 1940, having published no part of his edition. Responsibility for it passed to Dr Alice Walker. She published valuable studies of Shakespeare's text, and worked on editions of two plays in Cambridge University Press's 'New Shakespeare'; but the edition that McKerrow had planned did not come into being. In the meantime, other editions of the plays were published, including the later volumes of the New Shakespeare (better known as the New Cambridge edition), the new Arden and New Penguin editions (so far incomplete), the single-volume unannotated editions of Peter Alexander (1951) and C. J. Sisson (1954), and (originating in America) the annotated single-volume Pelican (1969), Signet (1972), Craig–Bevington (1973), and Riverside (1974) editions. Work has been resumed on the New Variorum edition; an American old-spelling edition, to be known as the International Shakespeare, is in preparation, under the supervision of Professor J. Leeds Barroll; and since our own plans were under way, Cambridge has embarked upon a new multi-volume edition, under the General Editorship of Professor Philip Brockbank.

McKerrow himself provided some justification for this apparent duplication of labour in the first sentence of his *Prolegomena*: 'there might, I suppose, be at least half a dozen editions of the works of

Shakespeare executed on quite different lines, each of which, to one
group of readers, would be the best edition possible.' To this we
must add the fact of mutability. Editions grow out of date in various
ways. New textual theories are propounded; scholarly discoveries
are made; ways of reading Shakespeare change.

*   *   *

The newly proposed Oxford editions will be in modern spelling.
This procedure, traditional in editions of Shakespeare, removes
unnecessary barriers to understanding, making it possible for the
reader to concentrate on the text itself, undistracted by obsolete and
archaic accidentals of presentation. Thus, his reading experience is
closer to that of Shakespeare's contemporaries, who also read the
plays in what was, for them, a modern form. We plan both a new
single-volume edition of Shakespeare's works for the Oxford
Standard Authors (OSA) series, and a detailed scholarly edition,
devoting a volume to each play, for the Oxford English Texts
(OET). To justify this decision in detail would be over-laborious,
and would require us both to engage in the unwelcome and
ungrateful task of finding fault with a large body of generally
admirable work and immodestly to point to ways in which we think
we can do better. Suffice it to say that we shall be well pleased if we
can serve the next generation as well as we have been served by the
scholars from whose work we have learned, and on which we build.

McKerrow wrote in the Preface to his *Prolegomena* that 'apart
from a few pages contained in the prefaces to the older "Cambridge" edition of 1863-6, and Professor Dover Wilson's "Textual
Introduction" to the "New Cambridge Shakespeare" which
appeared in the edition of *The Tempest* in 1921, there seems to be no
connected discussion of the problems which confront the Shakespearian editor . . .'. Since then, much more has been written, and
editorial procedures are in many ways well defined. Those which I
have outlined for Oxford editors are in some respects no more than
a reassertion, with individual emphases, of accepted principles. But
it is remarkable that, although scholarly and popular editions in
modern spelling of works by Shakespeare and his contemporaries
abound, no detailed attempt seems to have been made to rationalize
the principles according to which the modernizing process is carried
out. It seemed to me therefore that my first task as General Editor of
a proposed new edition should be to make this attempt. It is printed

here in advance of the edition itself in the hope of stimulating discussion on a topic of interest not only to Shakespeare scholars but more generally to editors, students, and readers of English Renaissance texts.

There is, on the other hand, no lack of discussion of the principles by which editors may hope to approach ever closer to the words that Shakespeare wrote. Many important and detailed bibliographical investigations have been undertaken in the forty years since McKerrow's *Prolegomena* appeared. To some extent their effect has been to increase awareness of ignorance; we know that the concept of a definitive text is ultimately a will o' the wisp. But these and other studies have helped to show that real progress can be made in certain areas. They have revealed ways in which we can purge the texts of inauthentic accretions, and they have helped in the formulation of principles according to which we may choose among variant readings with greater confidence than our predecessors. They have also pointed the way forward, showing that problems of immediate relevance to the editorial task remain relatively unexplored, and suggesting ways in which they may be tackled. Some of the most editorially complex plays are those of which there are bad quartos, so in this area, too, it has seemed desirable to explore afresh a fundamental problem, as Gary Taylor has done in the three essays included in this volume. The 1600 edition of *Henry V* is, as he demonstrates, something of a special case among bad quartos. But his studies in relation to that play of the problems of contaminated transmission, of theatrical revision, and of the variable but nevertheless real authority of a memorial text are relevant not only to *Henry V* but more generally to the task of editing Shakespeare and contemporary dramatists.

Act, scene, and line references to Shakespeare's plays are to Peter Alexander's one-volume edition (1951). 'Through line numbers' are from the Norton facsimile of the First Folio (1968). We gratefully acknowledge advice and criticism from our Textual Adviser, Mr G. R. Proudfoot, and from Dame Helen Gardner, Professors David Bradley, Norman Davis, Kenneth Muir, H. J. Oliver, and G. W. Williams, Dr Thomas Berger, Dr Peter W. M. Blayney, and Mrs Lesley Burnett. And we are constantly aware of a debt to our predecessors within the Press, the late R. B. McKerrow, and Dr Alice Walker.

S. W. W.

TABLE OF CONTENTS

MODERNIZING SHAKESPEARE'S SPELLING
STANLEY WELLS   3

Semantically Indifferent Variants   6

Semantically Significant Variants   10

Exceptions   13

Contractions, Elisions, and Metrical Markings   18

Proper Names   27

Punctuation   31

Index of Words Discussed   35

THE TEXT OF *HENRY V*: Three Studies
GARY TAYLOR

Introduction   39

QUARTO COPY FOR THE FOLIO TEXT: A REFUTATION   41

WE HAPPY FEW: THE 1600 ABRIDGEMENT   72

Appendix A. Cast Chart for the Quarto Text: Eleven Actors   112

Appendix B. Cast Chart for the Quarto Text: Twelve Actors   117

Appendix C. W. W. Greg and *The Battle of Alcazar*   120

CORRUPTION AND AUTHORITY IN THE BAD QUARTO   124

Postscript: Implications   163

Modernizing
Shakespeare's Spelling

MODERNIZING
SHAKESPEARE'S SPELLING

THE practice of modernizing the spelling of Shakespeare and his contemporaries is an ancient one. It was followed to some extent as early as the First Folio, purely as a matter of printing-house practice. For centuries after this no one seems to have thought very seriously about it. W. J. Craig, in a Preface, dated 1894, to the earlier Oxford Shakespeare, wrote simply 'For the uncertain orthography of the old editions I have substituted the recognized orthography of the present day. But metrical considerations occasionally render the retention of the older spelling necessary, and I have deemed it desirable to adhere to the older forms of a few words which modern orthography has practically shaped anew.' Craig, like his predecessors and many of his successors, felt no need to justify the practice itself. More recently, its validity has become a topic of scholarly debate, attacked by some, defended by others. The opposing points of view were expressed in articles well known to scholars, John Russell Brown's 'The Rationale of Old-Spelling Editions of the Plays of Shakespeare and his Contemporaries', and Arthur Brown's 'A Rejoinder' (*Studies in Bibliography*, 13 (1960), 49–67, 69–76).

The argument about the scholarly validity of the practice itself has been attended by surprisingly little discussion of how, once modernization has been decided upon as a course, it should be carried out.[1] The assumption appears frequently to have been that it is, as an eminent bibliographer said to me after I told him of our plans, 'merely a secretarial task'. Anyone who has himself attempted to modernize the spelling of an Elizabethan author in

---

[1] The most important contribution is Jürgen Schäfer's 'The Orthography of Proper Names in Modern-spelling Editions of Shakespeare' (*Studies in Bibliography*, 23 (1970), 1–19; see pp. 27–31 below). Fredson Bowers expresses his own sympathy with 'complete and absolute' rather than partial modernization in 'Principle and Practice in the Editing of Early Dramatic Texts', in *Textual and Literary Criticism*, Cambridge, 1959, etc. He also remarks that 'editors engaged in modernisations of texts would be well advised to discuss their difficulties more fully in print for their mutual advantage and the formulation of some working conventions that will do the least damage. The guidance that single editors of recent Elizabethan series have received from general editorial instructions both in England and in America has certainly been insufficient' (p. 180).

a responsible fashion is likely to know that in fact it calls for many delicate decisions.

Perhaps the absence of extended theoretical discussion explains why there is much variation of practice from one edition to another, even from play to play within a single edition. Dover Wilson, whose edition began to appear in 1921, was fairly traditional in his adoption of modern forms. G. L. Kittredge, in 1936, was more disposed to retain archaic spellings. In the new Arden edition, published from 1951 onwards, practice varies considerably. Some editors, particularly in plays published during the 1950s, are highly conservative of old spellings; others have been more willing to modernize. All seem reckless by comparison with G. Blakemore Evans in the Riverside, of 1974. I suspect that editors have been driven back to conservatism by an awareness both of the complexity of their task and of the absence of any agreed principles. In this essay I hope to explore some of the problems that arise, and to suggest ways in which they may be faced.

I start with an expression of my own point of view. I do not believe that there is any virtue in conscious conservation of archaic and obsolete spellings. I subscribe to Alice Walker's conviction that 'the advantage lies with the traditional practice of bringing spelling into line with current usage, since a gallimaufrey of ancient and modern contributes nothing to a critical appreciation of the differences between Elizabethan speech habits and ours'.[1] More specifically, I should like to dissociate Oxford policy from that enunciated by G. Blakemore Evans, who writes in the introductory essay to the Riverside edition:

an attempt has been made to preserve a selection of Elizabethan spelling forms that reflect, or may reflect, a distinctive contemporary pronunciation, both those that are invariant in the early printed texts and those that appear beside the spellings familiar today and so suggest possible variant pronunciations of single words. In the first category, examples may be found in such forms (including also proper names) as haberdepois (avoirdupois), fift or sixt (fifth or sixth), wrack (wreck); Birnan (Birnam), Bullingbrook (Bolingbroke), Callice (Calais), Dolphin (Dauphin), Roan (Rouen). In the second category: bankrout-bankrupt, conster-construe, embassador-ambassador, fadom-fathom, incestious-incestuous, renowm-renown, vild-vile. For words in this second category the present text, following the example of Kittredge, adopts on each occurrence the variant form that

[1] 'Some Editorial Principles (with special reference to *Henry V*)', *Studies in Bibliography*, 8 (1956), 111.

appears in the copy-text. Although the forms preserved may in many cases represent scribal or compositorial choices rather than Shakespeare's own preferences, such an approach nevertheless suggests the kind of linguistic climate in which he wrote and avoids the unhistorical and sometimes insensitive levelling that full-scale modernization (never consistent itself) imposes. It was believed, in short, that something valuable was to be gained by allowing, within limits, something of the variety and colour of the originals to survive the process of modernization. (p. 39)

I see no virtue in an attempt to suggest a 'kind of linguistic climate' (which was, of course, modern to Elizabethans). The preservation of 'a selection of Elizabethan spelling forms' has the practical disadvantage of creating a need for many more glosses than normal in a modern-spelling edition, most of them serving no purpose beyond a reassurance that the unfamiliar spelling in the text is not a misprint. A single opening of Riverside's *2 Henry IV*, for example, includes *kinreds*: kindreds, *idlely*: idly, *heckfers*: heifers, *Saint Albons*: St. Albans, and *chevalry*: chivalry. The policy also leads to eccentricity and the kind of obscurity that defeats the end of modernization. It is no part of our aim to enable the reader to reconstruct an Elizabethan pronunciation of the texts, whether through spelling or other means. On the other hand, we certainly wish to avoid 'insensitive levelling', and to make provision for special cases created by, for example, wordplay, scansion, and rhyme.

*   *   *

Editors of modern-spelling texts generally observe the principle that a word is spelt as it appears in the lemma in the *Oxford English Dictionary* for the entry in which the word is defined. But this principle is easier to enunciate than to put into practice. Many difficulties arise from the existence of variant Elizabethan spellings of what appears to be the same word. If the word is now obsolete it usually presents no problem and can be represented by the standard *OED* form, e.g. *peise, chopine, kecksy, sutler, eisell* (*OED*'s spelling, though in *Hamlet eisel* has become traditional). If the word is still in use, variant Elizabethan spellings create no problem when they are felt to be totally insignificant. For example, sixteenth-century spellings of 'carrot' include *carot, carote,* and *carotte*; but these are indifferent variants, and the word is properly represented in a modern-spelling edition by *carrot*.[1] Even in modern English, such variant spellings are permitted; for example, we may use 'grey' or 'gray' indifferently. But some variants have shades of significance even though there is no semantic difference. Thus, while in England *whisky* is now (as Fowler[2] says) 'the standard form', 'the Irish variety is usually spelt *-ey*', and this is the normal American spelling. Such shades of significance are more easily observed in a standardized spelling system than in a flexible one. When Elizabethan spelling variants may be suspected of having significance, an editor may feel a duty to retain, or standardize, them rather than use the accepted modern spelling. The kinds of significance that may attach to various forms are numerous. In the following sections I shall attempt to distinguish various categories of words which may present problems. First, I consider variants which are semantically indifferent, then those which involve meaning.

SEMANTICALLY INDIFFERENT VARIANTS

Editors have frequently justified the retention of old spellings on the grounds that they represent differing 'forms' of words, but without clearly defining what they mean by 'form'. For example, J. C. Maxwell, in the new Arden *Titus Andronicus*, saying that he has 'retained all older forms that are more than variant spellings' (p. xvi), prints *banket* (for *banquet*); but *OED* treats this simply as a variant, contemporaneous spelling, with no difference in etymology or sense. Similarly, Peter Ure, in the new Arden *Richard II*, has 'retained such archaic forms as may reasonably be believed to be more than mere spelling variants' (p. xxvii), and cites, *inter alia*, *caitive* (for *caitiff*), *president* (for *precedent*), and *murthered* (for *murdered*). A few other examples of spellings which some editors have modernized, some not, are *fadom* (*fathom*), *burthen* (*burden*), *bile* (*boil*, sb.), *asprey* (*osprey*), *arrand* (*errand*), *accompt* (*account*), *venter* (*venture*), and *tottered* (*tattered*). Editors have been particularly reluctant to modernize when the variation is consonantal, e.g. *apricock* (*apricot*); *bankrout* (*bankrupt*); *margent* (*margin*).   It is

[1] A highly conservative editor might conceivably wish to retain other variant spellings, such as *caret*, *carrat*, and *carroote*, on the grounds that they could reflect 'a distinctive contemporary pronunciation'. (The word does not, in fact, occur in Shakespeare.)

[2] H. W. Fowler, *Modern English Usage*, second edition, revised by Sir Ernest Gowers, 1965, etc., s.v. 'whisky'.

sometimes suggested that spellings which give different consonants from modern forms should regularly be retained, yet few if any editors would wish to follow their control-text in retaining the *d* in *frendzies*, omitting the *b* in *limb*, or spelling *knive's* (for *knife's*).

In what sense, we may ask, can the old spellings of such words be regarded as variant 'forms that are more than variant spellings'? Many editors follow the rule of thumb that the existence of a separate entry in *OED* for a variant warrants considering that spelling as a distinct form; but in fact *OED* makes no clear distinction between spelling and form; old spellings are usually merely cross-referred to the main entry and listed as 'variants', 'variant forms', or 'obsolete forms'. Some have an entry to themselves: examples are *subtile* (perhaps more common as a current spelling when *OED* was prepared than now), of which almost all the meanings distinguished are identical with those for *subtle*, and which is etymologically undifferentiated; *vild*, stated to be a 'variant', 'with excrescent -d', 'common from *c*. 1580 to 1650'; and *swound* and *sound*, variant forms with excrescent -d of *swoune*, where the problem is complicated, at least in verse, by the fact that the past tense and past participial forms make two syllables as opposed to the monosyllabic *swooned*. But other words in which variations of spelling (or form) are no less, are listed in *OED* under a single entry, e.g. *apricot/apricock*, *porcupine/porpentine*, *sampire/samphire*, *shrieve/sheriff*.

It is clear, then, that the presence or absence in *OED* of a separate entry for a variant spelling affords no criterion by which variant forms can be distinguished from variant spellings of words in which there is no distinction of definition. Is any other criterion available? Sometimes the form of the control-text[1] represents an inflection now obsolete in standard English, e.g. *eyne*, or *eyen* (for *eyes*), *spake* (for *spoke*), *forsook* (p.p., for *forsaken*), *mistook* (p.p., for *mistaken*), *arose* (for *arisen*), *holp* (for *helped*). I should not alter these, as they are genuine forms, not variant spellings.

Some variants represent or suggest a variant pronunciation. Of course, sound is important in verse. But to retain some early spellings simply because the editor regards them as aurally

---

[1] I use the term 'control-text' to mean the most authoritative text, and therefore the one on which an edition will be based, permitting a distinction from 'copy-text', a term apparently invented by R. B. McKerrow (*Prolegomena for the Oxford Shakespeare*, Oxford, 1939, reprinted 1969, p. 12, n. 1), which is perhaps best reserved for a text which provides the principal source of incidental as well as substantive readings.

preferable is like playing occasional notes of a Beethoven sonata on a fortepiano while the rest are played on a modern grand piano; it adds phonetic confusion to orthographical inconsistency. There are several reasons for this. Many words whose spelling has not changed were formerly pronounced differently, as we can see in such Shakespearian rhymes as *can/swan* ('The Phoenix and the Turtle', ll. 14-15) and *intreats/frets* (*Venus and Adonis*, ll. 73-5). Moreover, Elizabethan English had its share of non-phonetic spellings, and it is naïve to suppose that spellings such as *buckrom, strook, St Albons,* and *sate* (which Shakespeare rhymes with *bat, gnat,* and *hat*)—all of which, incidentally, the Riverside editor adopts—necessarily convey the Elizabethan pronunciation of these words to a modern reader any more accurately than their modern equivalents. The fact that many spellings in early texts are compositorial, not authorial, is of only secondary importance. Only an edition in phonetic characters could indicate how the text would have sounded to Shakespeare's contemporaries; and even then it would represent only a selection from the wide range of pronunciations available at the time. With certain exceptions, which I will discuss later, I see no case for retaining the old spelling of a word simply on the grounds that this is, or may be, a guide to its pronunciation.

Another sense in which earlier 'forms' might be regarded as 'more than mere spelling variants' is that they may be held to represent a stage in a word's morphological development distinct enough from other stages to constitute a separate form. Some of these arise from the introduction of an etymological spelling, now abandoned; examples are *compt, accompt, conceipt, deceipt.* Such spellings do not necessarily reflect contemporary pronunciation; for example, 'deceipt' rhymes with 'repeat' at *Pericles* 1.4.75. Conversely, we have in early texts phonetic spellings, such as *ile, det,* and *detter,* of words for which we now use the etymological spelling (*isle, debt, debtor*). To retain the old spelling in these words would tell us simply how they were spelt by some people in Shakespeare's time, a function quite outside the scope of a modern-spelling edition.

Other variants result from the influence of foreign-language forms. For example, *apricock* derives from Portuguese or Spanish; *apricot,* from the cognate French word. Only the former occurs in early texts of Shakespeare, though the latter was also used in the period. Rather similar is *bankrout/bankrupt.* Both forms are found in early texts of Shakespeare, though *bankrupt* only in the Folio, which may suggest that it was regarded as a modernization. To preserve the old spelling in these and similar cases would probably represent Shakespeare's own preference: it might be of interest to a student of language. If it is felt to be an important distinction, it would be proper to note it, at least, in the Folio-only texts, if not to emend. But as no distinction of meaning is involved, and as we have no sense that Shakespeare was selecting one form rather than the other for special effect, I think that in these and similar cases the modern spelling is to be preferred in a modern-spelling edition.

It is perhaps easiest to make a distinction between spelling and form in aphetic and syncopated forms of words which affect the number of syllables. Thus, *stonish* has a distinct *OED* entry from *astonish*, and is described as an 'aphetic form' of *astonish*; *gainst*— 'also 'gainst'—is said to be 'Rather a poetic aphetizing of AGAINST than the direct descendant of GAIN, GAINS'; *limbeck* is 'aphetized from ALEMBIC'; *larum* is an 'Aphetic form of ALARUM'; *rest* occurs as an 'Aphetic form of *arest* ARREST'; *ignomy* is a 'Shortened form of IGNOMINY'; and *canstick* is 'apparently a contracted form of CANDLESTICK' (to which, in *1 Henry IV* (3.1.131), it was altered, in despite of metre, in the First Folio). Clearly such forms affect the metre in verse, and they seem significant variants in that they have a colloquial quality. I think they should be preserved in a modern-spelling edition. It is not always clear whether they should be regarded as independent forms or as contractions, needing an apostrophe (see also Contractions, pp. 18–27 below). In cases of doubt, it seems helpful to the modern reader to print an apostrophe.

Besides shortened forms, we also have lengthened ones, such as *vild* and *swound*, mentioned above. I know of no evidence that these were felt to be in any sense (e.g. dialectally or colloquially) significant, so I should use the modern form.

Some variant Elizabethan spellings remain in use today alongside more standard spellings. For example, *OED* and its more recent derivatives give *corse* as a 'somewhat archaic and poetic form of *corpse*'; *hostler* is said to have 'always varied with the form OSTLER, now more prevalent', and is listed in the *Concise Oxford Dictionary* (new edition, 1976) with a cross-reference to *ostler*, though there the note '[earlier hostler]' seems to imply that by this date it is no longer felt to be a current form—and it is not listed at all in the *Oxford Advanced Learner's Dictionary of Current English*, perhaps a sign that it is obsolescent, in which case it resembles *subtile* (see p. 7 above). When there is no distinction in meaning, it seems right in modernizing to use the standard rather than the archaic form.

SEMANTICALLY SIGNIFICANT VARIANTS

I turn now to variant spellings which may appear to be semantically significant. In Shakespeare's time variant spellings of some words were used indiscriminately for variant senses which are still current, but in later times certain spellings have come to be attached to specific senses. *Courtesy* is an example. 'In the 16th c.', says *OED*, 'the medial short *e* was frequently elided, giving *court'sy*, *curt'sy*, formerly occasional in all senses, but now confined to 9 [i.e. an obeisance], and treated as a separate word: see CURTSY'. The modern-spelling editor faces several problems.

In verse, Shakespeare usually represents the modern sense, *courtesy*, with a form which is metrically trisyllabic, e.g. 'I thank you for your pains and courtesy' (*Julius Caesar* 2.2.115), but in *King Lear* we have 'Effects of courtesy [curtesie in Qq and F], dues of gratitude' (2.4.178). Most, if not all, editors spell this out in full, presumably regarding it as a word which can naturally be elided into a disyllable. This seems acceptable. (See also Elisions, pp. 18–27 below.) Sometimes it is not clear which sense is intended, e.g. (in prose), 'Pray you, leave your courtesy, good mounsieur' [curtsie Q1, courtesie Q2, F1] (*A Midsummer Night's Dream* 4.1.19), where the word could be used in the generalized sense of modern *courtesy* or the more particularized sense attached to modern *curtsy*, though with the broader meaning of an obeisance performed by males as well as females. Modern editors vary between the two forms, influenced no doubt by their interpretation of meaning.

Early editions also use a form lacking the medial 't', as in *The Merchant of Venice*, in a prose passage: 'He was wont to lend money for a Christian [cursie Q1, curtsie Q2, F]' (3.1.40–1). Here, although Q1 is the control-text, editors range the full gamut: *cursy* (Craig-Bevington), *cur'sy* (J. R. Brown (new Arden), Riverside), *curtsy* (J. Dover Wilson, glossing 'polite bow'), and *courtesy* (Peter Alexander, W. M. Merchant (New Penguin)). Again, interpretation enters into the question. Brown glosses 'a current form of curtsy or courtesy: these were, in fact, one word with a wide range of meanings—that of an act of generosity or benevolence may be most appropriate here'. Whatever the editor's interpretation of meaning, it seems to me that the absence of medial 't' is simply a spelling variant, so that the choice lies only between *courtesy* and *curtsy*.

The word occurs as a verb in a verse line in *Titus Andronicus* ('And shee whom mightie kingdomes cursie too', 5.3.74; 'cursie' in both Q1 and F1). Dover Wilson spells *curt'sy*; the apostrophe is redundant. W. J. Craig, Peter Alexander, and the Pelican editor (Gustav Cross) more logically spell *curtsy*, the modern form for this sense. J. C. Maxwell (new Arden) reverts to *cur'sy*, noting 'this phonetic spelling . . . seems worth preserving.' His practice is open to the objections noted on pp. 7–8. Craig–Bevington's *court'sy* seems quite mistaken in bringing the control-text's spelling closer to that of the modern noun, rather than the verb as the sense requires.

Other examples, also common in Shakespeare, are *metal/mettle* and *travel/travail*, used without distinction of either spelling or meaning in the early editions. It seems right for the modern editor to adopt the modern distinction of spelling for variant meanings. Sometimes Shakespeare's use is significantly ambiguous (e.g. *Julius Caesar* 1.2.307–8, 'yet I see, / Thy Honorable Mettle may be wrought', F1). In such cases it is most helpful to adopt the spelling of the primary sense, and annotate.

A slightly different situation arises with words of which there were variant Elizabethan spellings, used indifferently and now standardized, and which have narrowed in range of meaning. An example is *quote*, also spelt *coat(e)*, *cote*. *Cote* is listed in *OED* (*v.*[3]) simply as a variant of *quote*. Shakespeare uses it in different obsolete senses, e.g. *Love's Labour's Lost*, 'His face's own margin did quote such amazes' (2.1.245), *King John*, 'A fellow . . . / Quoted . . . to do a deed of shame' (4.2.221–2), etc. Riverside preserves *cote* when this is the control-text's spelling, but most other editors spell *quote*, which seems right since the word will have to be glossed anyway, and also because it helps to preserve the distinction from the genuinely different *cote* (*OED v.*[1], now obsolete), meaning 'pass by', 'outstrip', as used in *Hamlet* ('We coted them on the way', 2.2.315).

Sometimes modern spelling distinguishes senses which were orthographically indistinct to Shakespeare's contemporaries. For example, *wrack(e)* was used for senses now shared between *wreck* and *wrack*. A modern editor does best to use the spelling now current for the dominant sense. Thus, at *Henry V* 4.1.97, 'Euen as men wrackt vpon a Sand' (F1), I should spell 'wrecked', but at *Henry V* 1.2.164–5, 'As is the Owse and bottome of the Sea / With sunken Wrack' (F1), I should retain *wrack* in the sense 'wreckage' (*OED* wrack *sb.*²1.b).

An ultimately insoluble problem arises when it is not possible to identify a dominant sense (this is perhaps the most serious objection to modernizing spelling). So it may be with 'humane', used in Shakespeare's time for both senses that we now distinguish, in spelling and pronunciation, as *human* and *humane* (e.g. 'Ere humane Statute purg'd the gentle Weale', *Macbeth* 3.4.76, F1) with *diuers/diuerse* used indifferently for senses that are now distinguished (as in 'diuide / The state of man in diuers functions', *Henry V* 1.2.184), and with a few other words. In such cases the editor can only, after weighing the evidence, make an arbitrary decision, while annotating the alternative interpretation.

Some words which are etymologically distinct were confused in the Elizabethan period and spelt identically, but are now kept apart. An example is *ingenious/ingenuous*; it is complicated by the fact that some senses are now obsolete. For example,

A course of Learning, and ingenious studies
(*The Taming of the Shrew* 1.1.9)

where *ingenious* is used 'by confusion for INGENUOUS' in *OED*'s obsolete sense 'Of employment or education, etc.: Befitting a well-born person; "liberal"'. In *Cymbeline*, the reverse confusion occurs:

My ingenuous Instrument   (4.2.187)

where the word is used in *OED*'s definition of *ingenious* I.3.b, 'showing cleverness of invention or construction; skilfully or curiously contrived or made'. In these cases, my opinion is that the word should be spelt in the way which corresponds to *OED*'s spelling representing the meaning required, whether this meaning is obsolete or not. Thus, in *The Taming of the Shrew* I should spell *ingenuous*, and in *Cymbeline*, *ingenious*. This may savour of correcting Shakespeare, but there seems to have been no sense in the sixteenth century that the one word was mistakenly used for the other, so they may be regarded simply as spelling variants of a single word that had many different senses, which puts them essentially in the same category as those words treated on pp. 10-11.

Another category of words is those in which the spelling of the control-text indicates a distinction of sense recognized at the time of composition but now subsumed in the modern form. Examples are *mo* (or *moe*), used by Shakespeare and his contemporaries to mean 'more in number', and *enow*, used as the plural of *enough*. A case could be made for placing these in the same category as obsolete inflexions; but the distinction is not regularly observed in the early editions (e.g. 'We haue willing Dames enough', *Macbeth* 4.3.73, F1; 'Sing no more ditties, sing no moe', *Much Ado About Nothing* 2.3.65, Q1), which suggests that it was already weakening. Furthermore, preservation of the old spelling cannot inform the modern reader of the old distinction. Where the modern word can be used in the sense distinguished in the old spelling, I see no case for not modernizing.

EXCEPTIONS

The following paragraphs treat of instances in which it may be desirable to retain original spellings (or to standardize them) for special reasons.

Some characters in Shakespeare's plays are represented as speaking a conventionalized stage dialect, as in the exchanges between Edgar and Oswald, in *King Lear* 4.6. Here and elsewhere, the original spellings have to be retained or adapted in a way which will convey their import to a modern reader or actor. I see no point in going to great lengths to retain every spelling that may possibly be interpreted as an indication of dialectal idiosyncrasy of pronunciation, especially when this may cause bewilderment. As G. L. Brook writes (in a useful chapter on 'Dialects, Registers and Idiolects', *The Language of Shakespeare*, 1976), 'Shakespeare's use of dialect is sketchy and conventional, consisting of a few hints to the actor' (p. 177). This, along with the possibility of scribal or compositorial contamination, justifies us in not treating the original texts as if they were a William Barnes-like attempt at a phonetic representation of speech. So, in *The Merchant of Venice* 2.2.147, I should be inclined to alter Launcelot's *a leuen* (Q1, F1; *eleuen* Q2) to *eleven* (as do Dover Wilson and W. M. Merchant (New Penguin)) rather than to print *a 'leven* (W. J. Craig) or *aleven* (J. R. Brown (new Arden), Riverside), particularly since *OED* gives *aleven* as a normal sixteenth-century spelling, it is used by Hamlet (Q2, 1.2.251) (and by Emilia in the 'Shakespearian' part of *The Two Noble Kinsmen*) as well as by 'low-life' characters (Thersites, Costard, Juliet's Nurse, the Clown in *The Winter's Tale*, and John Lincoln in *Sir Thomas More*), and since *aleven* does not convey dialectal significance to a modern reader, and would be of no help to an actor. On the other hand, the *ch* in Edgar's *cham* is simply an aphetic form of *ich*, the now-obsolete form of *I* and so is properly represented as *'ch*. I should follow similar principles in modernizing idiosyncratic spellings representing the speech of uneducated characters, foreigners, etc.

I do not think that dialectal spellings should be preserved merely on the grounds that they represent Shakespeare's own preferences. This may require some delicate decisions. For example, Joseph Wright, in his *English Dialect Dictionary* (6 vols., 1898–1905), gives *apricock* as a dialectal form of *apricot*, used in Warwickshire among other places. The consonantal ending is found in the early texts for Shakespeare's three uses of the word. In *Richard II* 3.4.29 ('Go bind thou vp yong dangling Aphricokes', Q1), the editor would be justified in retaining it if he felt that it was a characterizing touch for the Gardener, but not otherwise; he might in any case hesitate on observing the 'Aph-' beginning of the word—a spelling not recorded in *OED*—and considering that retention of the consonantal ending might also logically entail spelling *africocks*.

Sometimes the use of a form deriving from popular etymology may be interpreted as a characterizing touch (though there may be doubt whether it is a mere spelling variant, possibly scribal or compositorial, rather than an authorial choice). Thus, an editor might (or might not) wish to print *lanthorn* (for Q and F's *lanthorne*) if he regarded it as a characterizing touch for Dogberry (*Much Ado About Nothing* 3.3.21), but to modernize Henry VI's *Lanthorne* (F1, *2 Henry VI* 2.3.25) to *lantern* on the grounds that the King's diction is basically unidiosyncratic. So also with Hotspur's *Parmacitie* (Q1, Parmacity F1, *1 Henry IV* 1.3.58). *OED* has an entry for 'parmacety', described as 'a popular corruption of SPERMACETI', and noting *parmacetie* as a sixteenth-century form. A modernizing editor might therefore print *parmacety* as an adoption of a standard spelling of an obsolete word. This would not imply that there was anything characteristic about Hotspur's use of it. On the other hand, he might prefer to spell *parmacity* on the grounds that this form is further away from the 'learned' (particularly because, according to the new Arden editor, A. R. Humphreys, 'The spelling "parmacitie" or "parmacity" for "spermaceti" was apparently due to a fanciful etymology from "Parma city"'), and therefore more expressive of Hotspur's character. (Humphreys writes in his Introduction (p. lxxvii) that the word 'should not be pedanticized into "spermaceti"', which seems just, 'or bastardized into "parmaceti"', which seems to ignore *OED*'s acknowledgement of this as a common corruption.)

Occasionally a case can be made for departing from *OED*'s modern spelling when an old spelling helps the reader to see that a word is not what he might otherwise suppose; for example, *breeze* is *OED*'s spelling for the sense 'gadfly', as in *Troilus and Cressida* 1.3.48, 'The herd hath more annoyance by the breeze' (Bryze Q1, Brieze F1), but there is clearly a gain in adopting the traditional spelling *breese* (cf. Alice Walker, *Troilus and Cressida*, New Shakespeare edition, p. 132: 'The spelling of the text is that of the relevant *OED* main entry except in a few cases where a distinctive traditional spelling has obvious advantages: e.g. *breese* = gadfly (*OED* 'breeze'), *empale* = surround (*OED* 'impale')'). Another example is provided by *silly*. The variant *seely* has a separate *OED* entry, but 'silly' is described simply as 'Later form of ME. sely SEELY a', and there are no essential differences of definition. Nevertheless, the old form may usefully be preserved as a way of drawing attention to the obsolete meaning, or of attempting to eliminate unwanted modern associations, as at *The Rape of Lucrece* 1345, 1812, and *Richard II* 5.5.25. This spelling should also then be adopted when the control-text reads *silly* if the obsolete meaning is clearly dominant.

Problems occur when objects have greatly changed but names remain. Logic suggests that even in these cases the modern spelling should be used. Often it cannot be avoided. After all, when Falstaff speaks of a 'cup of sack' he certainly does not allude to anything that most modern readers would think of as a 'cup'; but there is no alternative spelling that would arouse more appropriate associations. When such an alternative does exist the temptation to use it is great. An example is the word represented in *OED* by the entry 'hautboy, hoboy'. There is a separate entry for *oboe*, which came into English through the Italian in the eighteenth century. The Elizabethan musical instrument was different from the modern one, and although the words are etymologically related, some purpose may be served by keeping the words distinct. *Sherris* also has a distinct *OED* entry from *sherry* but is marked as archaic. *Sherry* is stated to be a singular form 'evolved from SHERRIS, mistaken for a plural'. For this reason, and because the drinks appear to have differed in character, Falstaff may be allowed to speak of 'sherris sack'.

Related to this is *sallet*, described by C. T. Onions in his *Shakespeare Glossary* (1911, etc.) as 'a prevalent Elizabethan form of "salad"' and with no distinct *OED* entry in this over-all sense. In Hamlet's 'no sallets in the lines to make the matter savoury' (2.2.434) its sense of 'something tasty' (C. T. Onions) makes 'salads' a misleading modernization, and W. J. Craig and Dover Wilson, for example, retain *sallets*, no doubt in order to avoid the associations of 'salad'. In *All's Well that Ends Well*, however, the word is used in a sense less distant from the modern: 'She's the sweet marjoram of the salad' (4.5.14), and here the same editors use the modern spelling, which seems right. (Still more complex is the passage in *2 Henry VI*, 4.10.7–15, which includes word-play on *sallet* = salad and *sallet* in the now obsolete sense of 'helmet', where retention of old spelling is justified by the word-play.)

Another 'distinctive traditional spelling' is *an* meaning 'if', though the tradition largely postdates Shakespeare. According to *OED*, 'Except in *an't*, *an* is found only once in the 1st Folio of Shakspere . . .; but modern editors substitute it for the full *and* usual in Shakspere and his contemporaries.' This practice is attacked by J. C. Maxwell in his new Arden edition of *Titus Andronicus*: 'I have also rejected what may be called pseudo-modernizations: forms that were modernizations when they became part of the accepted text but have lingered on although they are now just as obsolete as the forms they supplanted: a good example is "swounded" (V. i. 119). The most important word in this class is "and". In Elizabethan English "and" and "and if" were both used as equivalents of "if". In the course of the seventeenth century it became customary to write "an" instead of "and" in this sense, and "an" became universal in the eighteenth-century editions. But now that the usage is completely obsolete, it seems to me high time to return to the original spelling' (p. xvi).

It is not quite true that 'the usage is completely obsolete', as *an* is still current in the expression 'ifs and ans'; whichever form is used, a gloss is required; *an*, even if it is not truly a modern spelling, is less old in this sense than *and*, and it alerts the reader to the difference in meaning. For these reasons I should spell *an* when the meaning is clearly 'if', while retaining *and* in doubtful cases.

Sometimes a case can be made for retaining an old spelling in order to clarify word-play, as in

> This lanthorn doth the hornèd moon present
>
> (*A Midsummer Night's Dream* 5.1.233)

and

> He hath the horn of abundance . . . though he have his own lanthorn to light him.
>
> (*2 Henry IV* 1.2.42–5)

Metre, too, will often make its demands. It is necessary to retain the archaic *academe* in

> Our court shall be a little academe
> (*Love's Labour's Lost* 1.1.13)

Another word requiring exceptional treatment in verse is *thorough/ through* (indifferent variants; cf. p. 6 above), as in

> Over hill, over dale,
>   Thorough bush, thorough brier,
> Over park, over pale,
>   Thorough flood, thorough fire . . .
>
> (*A Midsummer Night's Dream* 2.1.2-5)

Deliberate archaisms, such as those in Gower's speeches, in *Pericles*, call for similar treatment.

   Rhyme, too, may have to be considered; and it often presents acute problems, to which only compromise solutions are possible. In many cases there is no way of spelling a word, in either old or modern spelling, that will suggest a rhyme in modern pronunciation; a few examples from *Venus and Adonis* are: *prove/love* (40-2); *slave/have* (101-2); *bounds/wounds* (265-7); *heaven/even* (493-5); *swine/groin* (1115-16); *bone/gone* (56-8); *ear/hair* (145-7); *fear/ there* (320-2); *grapes/mishaps* (601-3). If nothing can be done to show that these words once rhymed, the editor may wonder whether there is any point in retaining old spellings which do suggest a rhyme but may disconcert a reader, when modernization of spelling would produce collocations of words no more surprising than those for which he has no choice. Examples from *Venus and Adonis* are: *mouth/drouth* (542-4); *enter/venter* (626-8); *parasits/wits* (848-50); *further/murther* (905-6); *confess/decesse* (1001-2); *fraud/o'er strawed* (1141-3). Decisions will be subjective. Only in the last example does it seem to me essential to retain the old spelling, because there the grammatical form is involved. Nor should I necessarily wish to preserve *mo* (instead of 'more') rhyming with *so*; I think 'Sing no more ditties, sing no mo' looks ridiculous, and that *more/so* is no more violent in rhyme than *great/eat* (present tense) *forbear thee/near thee*, and *have/grave*, which we accept willy-nilly in 'Fear no more the heat o'th'sun' (*Cymbeline* 4.2.259-82). Grammatically, both occurrences of the word in this line serve the same function, so it seems illogical to spell them differently; and I cannot believe that Shakespeare would have expected a singer to make a distinction in sound between the first and second, as if to signal that a rhyme was coming up. (It would, nevertheless, be possible to argue either that the ludicrous effect is intentional, or that Shakespeare has miscalculated.)

The modernizing editor is sometimes faced with a problem when he believes that the original spelling hints at a meaningful ambiguity. For example, Hilda Hulme (*Explorations in Shakespeare's Language*, 1962, repr. 1977, p. 237) refers to Banquo's

> My Noble Partner
> You greet with present Grace, and great prediction
> Of Noble hauing, and of Royall hope,
> That he seemes wrapt withall. . . .

> (*Macbeth* 1.3.54–7)

and comments that *wrapt* 'may contain more meaning than the usual modernisation "rapt" would suggest: as well as having relation to the imagery of "borrowed Robes" and "strange Garments" which follows, it may imply also Banquo's later judgment:

> oftentimes, to winne vs to our harme,
> The Instruments of Darknesse tell vs Truths. . . .

The word can mean "entangled, caught" or "implicated" . . .'. In such cases it seems best normally to adopt the modern spelling for the dominant meaning, and to annotate if the editor feels that additional resonances should be drawn to the reader's attention.

CONTRACTIONS, ELISIONS, AND METRICAL MARKINGS

I have said that we are not attempting to represent the way in which Shakespeare's texts may have been pronounced by his contemporaries. This statement requires some modification. The early texts contain clues as to how their author intended them to be spoken. Sometimes these clues are direct, as in the quasi-phonetic spelling of dialect passages. Sometimes they are indirect, as when they are deduced from the metre. Some may be classed as accidental, some as substantive. 'Substantive' matters of pronunciation include those affecting the scansion of verse lines; those indicative of personal idiosyncrasies in a dramatic character's speech: deviations from a norm—such as dialectal or colloquial spellings—which may be regarded as part of the dramatist's technique of characterization; and unusual word formations which may be deliberately chosen for the sake of euphony. Accidental matters may be more negatively defined as indications that a standard pronunciation of a word will in no way diminish the dramatic and poetic effect.

The distinguishing of substantive from accidental characteristics of pronunciation is often a highly subjective matter, and is complicated by problems in interpreting the evidence. Because Elizabethan spelling was far from phonemic, it is often difficult to be sure whether an idiosyncratic pronunciation was intended. There is always the danger that the evidence has been obscured in the process of transmission, by scribes and compositors. In addition to this, the modernizing editor has to decide what current orthographic conventions should be employed in the attempt to translate substantive indications of pronunciation into modern terms, and on the degree to which they should be made explicit.

The following paragraphs attempt to define some of the problems in more detail, and to suggest ways of dealing with them.

Editors have frequently emended Shakespeare's text in order to improve metre. Metrical changes include rearrangements in the order of words (e.g. Hanmer's 'Thy mistress I know not' for 'I know not thy mistress', *The Comedy of Errors* 2.1.68), omission of words (e.g. Pope's 'The nobles they are fled, the commons cold' for 'The nobles they are fled, the commons they are colde', *Richard II* 2.2.88, Q1), addition of words (e.g. Rowe's 'as much as to say' for 'as much to say', *The Comedy of Errors* 4.3.48, F1), and alteration of words (e.g. F2's ''gainst all exceptions' for 'against all exceptions', *Henry V* 4.2.25, F1). Such emendations may of course be justifiable, but they may also stem from misunderstandings about Shakespeare's language and of his metrics, and all traditional emendations of this kind need to be carefully re-examined.[1] The information that is gradually emerging as the result of studies of the habits of particular compositors may be relevant in the attempt to determine whether apparent metrical irregularity should be attributed to textual corruption.

The early texts include many contractions reflecting colloquial usage; editors have often thought that metre requires many more. It is quite possible that Shakespeare did not always indicate such

[1] I have found David Abercrombie's 'A Phonetician's View of Verse Structure', in his *Studies in Phonetics and Linguistics* (OUP, 1965, pp. 16–25), particularly helpful in relation to Shakespeare's metrics, especially in its emphasis on what he calls the 'stress-timed rhythm of English', which he finds to be 'the basis of the structure of English verse', as opposed to 'syllable-timed rhythm' (p. 18).

contractions orthographically. A. C. Partridge, who believes that Shakespeare's orthography can be discerned behind some of the early texts, writes on contraction between pronoun-subject and verb:

> the following quotations from *Richard II* (Q1), a precise play ortho-graphically, show that Shakespeare probably wrote out these combinations in full, relying on the actors to slur or syncopate them:
>
> II.1.7. Where words are scarce *they are* seldome spent in vaine
>
> V.6.28. For though mine enemy *thou hast* ever beene (unless *enemy* is disyllabic)
>
> Apparently Shakespeare continued thus until the turn of the century, when he began to abbreviate the pronoun. Quarto texts were often revised before the printing of the First Folio, as is illustrated by the following:
>
> 2 Henry IV, III.2.174. What, dost thou roare before *thou art* prickt? (prose; F1 *th'art*)
>
> (*Orthography in Shakespeare and Elizabethan Drama*, 1964, p. 63)

This probably does not make enough allowance for compositorial interference; nevertheless, it may serve as a warning against putting too much faith in the orthography of the early texts. It reminds us, too, that these are texts written to be spoken, in which the actor has some freedom to slur or elide in his own way. It is not the editor's responsibility to decide what this way should be. Although he may feel that the regular marking of elisions and contractions is helpful to the reader, it is wrong to follow the example of some earlier editors by cramming the text into a metrical strait-jacket. E. K. Chambers has an interesting discussion of elision, quoting A. W. Pollard's belief 'that elided syllables "should almost always be pronounced, but so lightly as not to interfere with the rhythm of the verse"'. Chambers has 'something of the same feeling myself. One retains some consciousness of the elided sound, but it does not amount to a metrical syllable.' But this is, he admits, 'a subtlety which we cannot expect typography to recognize' (*William Shakespeare*, i. 188–9). Some of the contractions introduced by editors are virtually unpronounceable, or suggestive of a pronunciation effectively indistinguishable from that of the full form. I prefer not to be over-subtle in the attempt to mark elisions, and to print the un-contracted form when this appears in the control-text, even if it requires to be elided or slurred, unless there is strong reason to suppose that exigencies of the printing-house have caused a compositor to expand it from an uncontracted form.

Conversely, early texts include contractions which editors have been tempted to expand for the sake of metre. G. L. Brook (§385) notes the following as a possible example:

> *Glendower* Ile not have it alter'd.
> *Hotspur* Will not you?
>
> (*1 Henry IV* 3.1.116; 'Ile' in both Q1 and F1)

Pope altered 'Ile' to 'I will' and was followed in many editions, including some now current, such as the Pelican. A. R. Humphreys (new Arden) prints 'I'll', noting 'Glendower's Welsh tune can make "I'll" quite long enough', and points to several other instances of apparently unmetrical contractions in Glendower's speeches. But the line scans perfectly well if we stress 'not' and hear what David Abercrombie[1] calls a 'silent stress' between the two sentences. Here, as elsewhere, current opinion about Shakespeare's metrics would discourage the expansion of contractions in order to produce a uniformity that is merely syllabic.

Sometimes contractions may lead editors to make questionable emendations. For example, the Duke's final couplet in *As You Like It* reads, in F1,

> Proceed, proceed: wee'l begin these rights,
> As we do trust, they'l end in true delights.

Since F2, almost every editor has emended 'wee'l' to 'we will'. A few modern editors have reverted to the contraction; but it does not accord with the formality of the situation. 'We will', however, is feeble; and it is at least worth considering J. C. Maxwell's suggestion, in a review of the new Arden edition (*RES* N.S. 27 (1976), 344), that the compositor's error was one of omission, not contraction (the line is crowded), and that the correct reading is 'wee'l so begin these rights'. In general it seems desirable to preserve the control-texts' contractions, introducing apostrophes in accordance with normal modern usage, unless the contraction appears to be compositorial in origin.

There are exceptions. In early texts, unsounded medial *e* is sometimes omitted, e.g. in *fastned, battred*, possibly signifying

---

[1] Ibid., p. 20.

syncope of the vowel before the *n* or *r* in the inflexional ending itself (Partridge, p. 70). It is often difficult to be sure whether this is simply a spelling variant; more importantly, the difference in pronunciation seems non-substantive, so I favour printing the medial letter. More generally, when it is unclear whether a particular spelling indicates contraction or is merely an indifferent variant, it seems reasonable to use the full modern spelling.

In past participles the spelling *-ne* (e.g. *falne*, *stolne*) seems sometimes to have been used to indicate elision, but it may also be a straightforward spelling variant; the light pronunciation is often effected in modern speech irrespective of spelling, so this too may be considered as a non-substantive indication of pronunciation.

The ending of the second person singular of verbs is variously spelt *-st*, *-'st*, and *-est*. These spellings may often be scribal or compositorial, and it seems right to regularize them, in verse spelling out the ending in full if it is required by the metre, if not, spelling with an apostrophe except in certain words which in modern printing of old texts are generally spelt without either medial *e* or an apostrophe; these include the auxiliaries *canst*, *couldst*, *mayst*, *wouldst*, *shouldst*, *hadst*, and *didst*. In prose the ending may be spelt *-est* except in those words where usage permits spelling *-st* (i.e. without the apostrophe), and in cases where a shortened form in the control-text is taken to represent a colloquial pronunciation, when the apostrophe is needed.

In verse it is not always necessary to expand a short form when doing so produces syllabic regularity. For instance, editors have often expanded one or both of the contractions in Caliban's line

> Which thou tak'st from me: when thou cam'st first
> (*The Tempest* 1.2.332, F1; the contractions were
> not obviously required to justify the line)

But this seems a clear example of a line with a medial silent stress, so alteration aimed at producing ten syllables would be misguided.

Individual words, including *whether*, *ever*, *never*, and *over*, often appear in both contracted and uncontracted forms. The contraction is justifiable at e.g. *The Tempest* 5.1.111, 'Where thou bee'st he or no', where it may be represented by *Whe'er*. But Pope and later editors often emended uncontracted forms to produce syllabically regular lines (e.g. *King John* 1.1.134, 'Whether hadst thou rather be a Faulconbridge', in which Pope emended *Whether* to *Say*; *Measure for Measure* 2.2.183, 'To sinne, in louing vertue: neuer could the Strumpet', where Pope emended *neuer* to *ne'er*). If we recognize that Shakespeare's versification is not primarily syllabic, such uncontracted forms can be accommodated to the metre. The possibility that Shakespeare did not expect such words to be contracted is increased by the similar metrical effect of other words for which no standard contractions existed, e.g. *neither* in 'Neither haue I money, nor commodity' (*The Merchant of Venice* 1.1.178), which Pope emended to *Nor*.

The problem of contractions becomes particularly acute in some of Shakespeare's late plays. Partridge (p. 116) writes, for example, 'In the Folio texts of *Coriolanus* and *Antony and Cleopatra* there is observed a highly developed dramatic orthography, replete with contractions and elisions of all kinds, such as *a'th, and't, in't, to't, to'th'Capitoll, upon's, th'fire*, alongside of the more familiar *wee'l, they'l, y'are, hang'em, ha's, ta'ne*.' Partridge suggests that this may be explained by Shakespeare's having 'absorbed from others a new technique of colloquial clipping, and developed it independently' (as he thinks probable), or by the texts' having undergone scribal or editorial intervention.

Modern editorial practice with such passages has varied greatly. We may take for illustration a passage discussed by Partridge (p. 90), who writes that

it is more than probable that the more difficult elisions were never even contemplated. For instance, in the passage cited by Bridges [*Milton's Prosody*, p. 79] from *Antony and Cleopatra* to illustrate the loss of accent on prepositions before and after a weak syllabic line of three accents, the full forms intended by Shakespeare are correctly given:

> We must return *to the* court of guard: the night
> Is shiny; and, they say, we shall embattle
> *By the* second hour, *in the morn.*
>
> (IV. 9. 2–4—Bridges has modernized spelling
> and punctuation)

In the First Folio this reads

> We must returne *to'th'* Court of Guard: the night
> Is shiny, and they say, we shall embattaile
> *By'th'* second houre *i'th* Morne.

No reputable actor would dare to clip the prepositional phrases in this fashion, nor is the prompter likely to have ordained such a notation for any seasoned member of his Company. If this is one of the plays directly printed from Shakespeare's manuscript, there was editorial interference in the process.

(Partridge's confidence in editorial interference here seems at odds with his already-quoted view that the Folio spellings reflect Shakespeare's 'new technique of colloquial clipping'.)

In this passage, as in others, examination of selected modernized texts shows an increasing conservatism over the past century or so. The Globe (1864), W. J. Craig (1891), old (1906), and new Arden (1954), read *to the*, *By the*, and *i'the*. In 1936, however, Kittredge had printed *to th'*, *By th'*, and *i'th'*. Dover Wilson did the same in 1950; so did Alexander in 1951, Pelican, Craig–Bevington, Riverside, and New Penguin (1977).

A similar process may be observed in *Coriolanus* 3.3.32–3. Folio reads:

> I, as an Hostler, that fourth poorest peece
> Will beare the Knave by'th Volume:
> Th'honor'd Goddes . . .

Globe, W. J. Craig, old Arden (1922) read:

> Ay, as an ostler, that for the poorest piece
> Will bear the knave by the volume. The honour'd gods . . .

Kittredge was conservative:

> Ay, as an hostler, that for th'poorest piece
> Will bear the knave by th'volume. Th'honour'd gods . . .

Alexander, Dover Wilson (in 1960), Craig–Bevington, Riverside, New Penguin (1967), and new Arden (1976) also retained all the Folio elisions. None of these editors retains the apostrophe in *by'*, which appears to be either a compositorial idiosyncrasy or an example of what Partridge (p. 93) calls 'Jonsonian elision', a 'metrical fiction, designed to indicate the desirability of retaining the full forms in reading'.

The 'clippings' found in the passages cited above, such as *o'*, *i'*, *th'*, and *t'* (= *to*), were 'in regular employment. They appear in prose to season the speech of garrulous characters like Pandarus . . .' (Partridge, p. 97). Clearly it would be inconsistent to expand contracted forms here yet retain them elsewhere, and the case for retaining them in late, Folio-only plays for which the printer's copy is believed to have been holograph is even stronger than elsewhere.

There seems no point, however, in printing the apostrophe after *By* in the lines from *Antony and Cleopatra*, as it would be meaningless to both a reader and a speaker.

Another common clipping is *a*, for *he*. There is no wholly satisfactory way of representing this typographically: with its Cockney associations, *'e* would give quite the wrong impression; and *'a* is not entirely happy, since the form is not an abbreviation of a modern (or any other) word, it obtrudes itself upon the reader's attention, and actors sometimes over-conscientiously try to represent the spelling in sound, with hiccoughing effect, instead of simply treating it as an unaccented form of *he*. The objection to *a* is that it is not a modern usage, and that it draws attention to itself, whereas what is wanted is some way of indicating that the pronoun is *not* emphatic. But *a* seems the least unsatisfactory way of continuing to indicate the control-text's distinction from *he*. When *a* appears as the 'worn-down form of "of" and "on"' (Onions), it is most helpfully replaced by *o'* unless *a* is still current, as in 'a tiptoe' (*Henry V* 4.3.42).

In Shakespeare's time the syllabic value of some words was variable. *Leprous*, for example, could be trisyllabic, *sulphurous* could be disyllabic. Here, as elsewhere, spelling is not necessarily indicative of pronunciation. It seems to me that each instance of this kind should be individually considered, with the proviso that the ordinary modern spelling should be adopted wherever it is not misleading. For example, *Hamlet* 1.5.64:

> The leaprous distilment, whose effect   (Q2)
>
> The leaperous Distilment; whose effect   (F1)

Here, I should adopt the old spelling *leperous* as the modern form is metrically misleading. (See also Spelling, Exceptions, p. 17.) The old spelling conveniently indicates the syllabic value required. This is not always available, as in the disyllabic pronunciation of the ending *-ion*, more common in Shakespeare's early than in his later plays (Partridge, p. 100). A diaeresis could indicate this, but as it might seem over-emphatic the pronunciation is perhaps best left to the reader's intelligence.

At *Hamlet* 1.5.3:

> When I to [sulphrus Q2; sulphurous F1] and tormenting flames

I should use the modern spelling (as in F1) as this can easily be accommodated to the metre (see also pp. 20–1 above).

A special case arises with inflected endings which have become contracted since Shakespeare's time. These do not quite fall into the category of obsolete inflections (see p. 7 above), since the inflection remains in modern English even if the ending does not form a separate syllable and is represented by a different spelling.

The commonest example in Shakespeare is the past tense and past participial ending -ed (sometimes also represented in early texts by -t and -d). This is sometimes sounded, sometimes not. It has become conventional in modernized texts to distinguish between the syncopated and the unsyncopated forms in one of two ways. Some editors represent the syncopated form by -'d and the unsyncopated by -ed, thus:

> Some shall be pardon'd and some punished.

Others represent the syncopated form by -ed and the unsyncopated form by -èd or -éd:

> Some shall be pardoned and some punishèd.

The former method has the disadvantage that the modern reader would not expect either *pardoned* or *punished* to be trisyllabic, and so does not need the apostrophe in *pardon'd* and could easily misread *punished* as disyllabic. The latter method has the disadvantage of drawing attention to itself as a typographical device, but the merit of drawing attention to the only word which requires a syllabification different from the modern. I prefer it for this reason. In prose there seems generally to be no reason not to print the normal modern form.

Obsolete comparatives form a related case. The old comparative *farre* occurs, as in 'Farre then Deucalion off' (*The Winter's Tale* 4.4.423); we also sometimes find *neere* as a comparative: 'Better farre off, then neere, be ne're the neere' (*Richard II* 5.1.88). *Farre* probably has to remain, as an obsolete word; *near* (for 'neere'), here used as a comparative, also requires to be treated as an obsolete form requiring a note or gloss. Editors need to be alert to the possibility that apparently positive forms are actually comparative, as perhaps at 1.2.109 in *The Winter's Tale*, 'To mingle friendship farre, is mingling bloods.'

When a contraction is to be retained, the editor may have a choice of spellings. So, in *The Merry Wives of Windsor*, 3.3.82–3, we have (in F1), 'You'r sham'd, y'are ouerthrowne, y'are vndone for euer.' Partridge writes (p. 98, n. 1), 'It is instructive to compare such alternative representations of combined contractions as *th'art* and *thou'rt*, *y'are* and *you're*, *th'are* and *they're*. The first is, in each pair, the commoner, but it may well be that no difference existed phonetically, and that the different orthographies were simply printers' or scribes' conventions.' Even if any difference did exist phonetically it would be, in my terms, 'accidental', so I think the standard modern forms, *thou'rt*, *you're*, *they're*, etc., should always be adopted in a modern-spelling text.

It is possible to be misled into thinking that a spelling is a contraction when in fact it can equally be regarded as a representation of a word's full form. For example, *deule* is sometimes regarded as a contraction of *devil*, and is so regarded by the Riverside editor, who prints *dev'l* even in *Sir Thomas More* where the metre requires disyllabic pronunciation:

> To lead those that the [devil] cannot rule.   (l. 53)

This is an additional warning that spelling may be conventional, not phonetic; *OED* records monosyllabic as well as disyllabic forms in the sixteenth and seventeenth centuries, and it was possible to write or print one while intending the pronunciation suggested by the other.

Sometimes a word becomes, as it were, lost in another. Thus, in *Measure for Measure* we have 'Words against mee? this 'a good Fryer belike' (5.1.131; F1). Here the common editorial practice of placing an apostrophe after 'this' (rather than before 'a' as in F1) provides a useful hint to the reader and the actor. Abbott[1] (§ 461) gives other instances of this assimilation (he wrongly states that F1 reads 'This' for 'This is' at *The Tempest* 4.1.143). When the spelling occurs in full, but metre suggests assimilation, as in Lear's 'This is a dull sight' (5.3.282), it seems best to spell in full since the phrase can be slurred in speech.

PROPER NAMES

I subscribe whole-heartedly to the principles of modernizing proper names propounded in Jürgen Schäfer's 'The Orthography of Proper Names in Modern-spelling Editions of Shakespeare' (*Studies in Bibliography*, 23 (1970), 1–19). Essentially, these should be no different from those applying to common nouns, but special problems

---

[1] E. A. Abbott, *A Shakespearian Grammar*, second edition, 1870, etc.

arise, particularly as *OED* is badly deficient in this area, so it seems worth looking at them separately.

Normally, adoption of the modern form of the name seems right except where metre demands otherwise; thus *Bolingbroke* (for *Bullingbrooke*, etc.), *Gertrude* (for *Gertrard, Hamlet* Q2), *Caithness* (for *Cathness*), *Bristol* (for *Bristow*). I should not retain old forms simply because they suggest what I have described as 'accidentals' of pronunciation. Nor do I see any force in G. K. Hunter's retention of *Birnan* (for *Birnam*) in his New Penguin edition of *Macbeth* on the grounds that Shakespeare's '*Birnan* is not the geographically precise modern Birnam' ('An Account of the Text', p. 189); the same might be said of London, or most other towns and countries, but is no justification for retaining old spelling in a modern-spelling text when the name clearly bears a close relationship to its modern geographical counterpart.

Some names have no corresponding modern forms outside texts of Shakespeare. In general they are best represented by the commonest spelling in the early texts, such as *Banquo*, or by a modernization of it such as omission of final, unsounded letters in *Fortinbras*[*se*]. Most such modernizations have become traditional, and there seems no reason to resist them as, for instance, G. K. Hunter resists *Goneril* (*King Lear*, New Penguin edition). This is *Gonorill* in Q, *Gonerill* in F. Hunter retains *Gonerill* because he knows 'of no relevant authority by which to correct it' ('An Account of the Text', p. 322); but *Goneril*, which appears to originate with Capell, is acceptable as a modernization in spelling analogous to *Florizel* (for *Florizell*) or *corporal* (for *corporall, Macbeth* 1.3.81). Another name whose traditional modernization seems acceptable is *Osric*, spelt *Ostricke* in Q2 and *Osricke* in F1 of *Hamlet*. It becomes *Osrick* in F3; *Osric* seems to originate with Isaac Reed. *Osricke-Osrick-Osric* is a straightforward process of modernization of the Folio spelling, so I see no reason against adopting *Osric* unless (as is quite likely) the editor thinks that the Q2 spelling has greater authority, in which case the appropriate modern spelling would seem to be *Ostric*.

The case for modernizing 'significant' proper names to the spelling of the corresponding common noun is discussed in detail in Schäfer's article. It seems right always to use the modern spelling of names such as 'Oatcake', 'Seacoal', etc., unless there is any reason to suppose that the original spelling is deliberately ambiguous or merely hints at a significance rather than proclaims it.

Sometimes the old form of a name is metrically preferable to the modern. When the old form is invariant, the editor's task is straightforward. So *Holmedon*, which occurs four times in *1 Henry IV*, and is always disyllabic, must be preferred to the modern *Homildon*, or *Humbleton*. Shortened, presumably colloquial, forms, used when the full form is metrically defensible, are less straightforward. Thus, in *Richard III* we have

At Pembroke, or at Harford-west [Q1; Hertford West F1] in Wales
(4.5.10)

The modern form *Haverfordwest* also existed in Shakespeare's time. It can be spoken, and an actor who can accommodate it to the metre might, in the interests of intelligibility, prefer to do so. But an editor, faced with evidence of a standard shortening, is likely to feel that he should indicate it. Most editors have printed *Ha'rfordwest*, which seems acceptable. Slightly more complex is *Ciceter* (in verse: *Richard II* 5.6.3). The modern spelling is *Cirencester*, but a pronunciation like that suggested by *Ciceter*, or *Cicester*, is still current in some circles. Nevertheless, *Cirencester* would lead most readers to misread the metre, even though it would make more sense geographically, so it seems best to adapt Q's spelling and print *Ci'cester*.

Sometimes an editor is faced with variant spellings which could also be regarded as metrically variant within a single text. It seems best to make them consistent unless a variant form is clearly idiosyncratic, or metrically misleading. For example, Q1 of *Richard II* (believed to be close to Shakespeare's manuscript) spells *Hereford* twenty-three times and *Herford* eleven times. There is no more strain in adopting *Hereford* to the metre when it is spelt so than when it is not, so I should regard alteration to *Herford* in these cases as an unwarrantable metrical emendation, and should regularly print *Hereford* for *Herford* as this is the modern spelling and is metrically defensible. I should admit, however, that this last is a knife-edge decision, and that a student would need a note to the effect that the medial *e* should be only lightly sounded.

Some names in Shakespeare (like some common nouns) call for syllabically different pronunciation on different occurrences. *Henry* sometimes apparently needs to be extended:

So stood the state when Henry the Sixth
(*Richard III* 2.3.16)

No reasonable spelling can indicate this; but it would be possible to print a diaeresis in

> And hollow pampered jades of Asïa
>
> (2 *Henry IV* 2.4.155)

Accepted anglicizations of foreign names, such as *Rome* (for *Roma*), *Milan* (for *Milano*), *Elsinore* (for *Helsingør*), or *Agincourt* (for *Azincourt*), often correspond to the Shakespearian form, and the standard practice of adopting them is obviously right. Often the Shakespearian (or contemporary) spelling is clearly an attempt to transliterate a foreign pronunciation. The second syllable of *Harflew* is an example. It corresponds to the modern *-fleur*, so I should not follow Kittredge and Blakemore Evans in retaining the Elizabethan spelling. Other examples are *Chatillion, Alanson, Rone* (or *Roan*), and *Callice*, properly modernized to *Chatillon, Alençon, Rouen*, and *Calais*. Early spelling may be retained in cases such as *Gaunt*, in *John of Gaunt*, where it has gained independent status: *John of Gaunt* is used by modern historians, even though *Gaunt* is not now accepted as an anglicization of *Ghent*.

Old spelling may have to be retained for metrical reasons, as with *Delabreth* in *Henry V*; the modern form, *D'Albret*, is metrically unacceptable:

> Charles Delabreth, High Constable of France   (3.5.40, 4.8.90)

More problematically, the place name *Marseilles* (*Marseille* in modern French) requires three syllables at *The Taming of the Shrew* 2.1.367:

> That now is lying in Marseilles road

and at *All's Well that Ends Well* 4.4.9-10:

> His grace is at Marseilles, to which place
> We have convenient convoy.

It also occurs in *All's Well* in prose (4.5.72). F1 (the control-text) spells *Marcellus* in the first and third instances, *Marcellae* (interpreted as a misprint for *Marcellus* by G. K. Hunter in his new Arden edition) in the second. The simplest course for a modern editor would be to retain F1's spelling, and annotate. F2 spells *Marsellis*. Judging by Sugden,[1] this was the commonest contemporary anglicization. It has the merit of preserving the metre, and at least

---

[1] Edward H. Sugden, *A Topographical Dictionary to the Works of Shakespeare and his Fellow Dramatists*, Manchester, 1925.

resembles the modern spelling more closely than *Marcellus*. Dover Wilson's *Marseillës* is rather uneasy as a compromise. Most modern editors print *Marseilles*, and this seems acceptable since modern English pronunciation (rhyming with *Wales*) can easily accommodate three syllables.

If no solution seems wholly satisfactory, one can only point to this as the kind of triviality over which editors agonize, changing their minds several times a day, rising from their beds to change it again, and telegraphing yet another vacillation to their sub-editors even after they have returned their final proofs. It is such anxieties, more perhaps even than major textual cruxes, that drive an editor to a state of impotent neurosis, or drink, or an early grave. The tossing of a coin at an early stage after all the pros and cons have been weighed, with a firm resolution to abide by its decision, may avert these calamities.

Occasionally, and oddly, a modern anglicization is metrically preferable to an early spelling: *Burgundy* gives us the three syllables required at *Henry V* 5.2.7, printed in F1 as:

We do salute you Duke of Burgogne.

PUNCTUATION

We do not know for certain to what extent the early texts reproduce Shakespeare's own punctuation. Nor can we confidently claim to understand all the nuances of Elizabethan practice. Certainly, the punctuation of the control-text would often bewilder or mislead a modern reader, and must be altered in a modern-spelling edition. In deciding what changes to make, the editor is likely to be influenced by his view of the authority of the punctuation in his control-text. If he believes that it indicates either how Shakespeare wished the lines to be spoken, or how the lines actually were spoken, he may wish to retain those of the supposedly rhetorical pointings whose significance is unchanged, and to replace the others by marks which would convey the same impression to the modern reader. If he lacks faith in the authority of the control-text's punctuation, he will have to adapt it to conform with some modern system, or to replace it with a modern system. Present-day practice is so flexible that in two different modernized editions the punctuation of parallel passages is likely to differ much more than the spelling. It is also likely to have

interpretative consequences. A few lines chosen at random will
illustrate this:

> Hang 'em! They say!
> They'll sit by th'fire, and presume to know
> What's done i'th'Capitol: who's like to rise,
> Who thrives, and who declines; side factions, and give out
> 5 Conjectural marriages; making parties strong,
> And feebling such as stand not in their liking
> Below their cobbled shoes. They say there's grain enough?
> Would the nobility lay aside their ruth,
> And let me use my sword, I'd make a quarry
> 10 With thousands of these quarter'd slaves, as high
> As I could pick my lance.

> (*Coriolanus*, new Arden edition, 1.1.189-99)

> Hang 'em! They say?
> They'll sit by th'fire and presume to know
> What's done i'th'Capitol, who's like to rise,
> Who thrives and who declines; side factions and give out
> 5 Conjectural marriages, making parties strong
> And feebling such as stand not in their liking
> Below their cobbled shoes. They say there's grain enough!
> Would the nobility lay aside their ruth
> And let me use my sword, I'd make a quarry
> 10 With thousands of these quartered slaves as high
> As I could pick my lance.

> (New Penguin edition)

The spelling is identical (except for one contraction), but there are
ten differences of punctuation in eleven lines. The new Arden editor
alters five of the Folio markings, the New Penguin, eleven. The
former system, it seems to me, is the more rhetorical, the latter, the
more grammatical (or logical). The medial commas in ll. 2, 4 (both
of them), 9 and 10 of the new Arden version all derive from the
Folio; the New Penguin editor rejects all but one of them. The
general effect is more jerky in the new Arden; it might be said to
convey more of a sense of the speaker's exasperated effort to find
words adequate to express his feelings. It also suggests breathings
which the actor might care to use. And several specific differences of
interpretation are suggested by the punctuation. The New Penguin
editor interprets F's exclamation mark after 'They say' as interroga-
tory, not exclamatory; Arden's retention of F's colon in l. 3 suggests
to a modern reader that 'who's like to rise', etc., is the result of
'what's done i'th'Capitol', whereas New Penguin's substitution of

a comma makes each noun clause depend on 'know'; Arden's substitution of a semi-colon for a comma in l. 5 destroys the sense of a causal connection between 'marriages' and 'making parties strong' which can be (but is not necessarily) obtained from the version with a comma; Arden retains the question mark after 'grain enough', but New Penguin interprets it as a mark of exclamation.

My intention in making these comparisons is not to suggest that one version is preferable to the other, but to point to the interpretative effect of punctuation, whether it is derived from a control-text or not, and to suggest that the editor should have firm confidence in the authenticity of the control-text's punctuation before he commits himself to attempting to convey its effect to the modern reader.

Michael J. Warren, in his article 'Repunctuation as Interpretation in Editions of Shakespeare' (*English Literary Renaissance*, 7.2 (Spring 1977), 155-69), valuably demonstrates that 'modern punctuation . . . has rhetorical implications, and its intrusion inevitably affects the phrasing and, especially for the actor, the intonation of the speech; the most innocent modernization may preclude an alternative interpretation, or alter a rhythmic pattern'.

But I cannot subscribe to his view that 'intelligent respect must be paid to the punctuation of original texts since nothing else has comparable authority, and that in editions that aspire to authoritativeness such punctuation must not be freely dismissed in favour of a modern substitute which is potentially confining, neutralizing, or distorting' (p. 157). This, it seems to me, makes too little allowance for the possibility that scribal, compositorial, or even editorial influence on the early texts may also have resulted in punctuation that is 'confining, neutralizing, or distorting'. We know that Folio punctuation tends to be heavier than that of the quartos; and there is ample evidence that compositors did not invariably follow the punctuation in their copy.

If the editor lacks faith in the authority of his control-text's punctuation he is left with the words alone. The aim, it seems to me, should be to give the reader and the actor such pointing as is essential to intelligibility without attempting to impose on the text interpretative nuances and directions for emphasis which restrict the reader's or actor's range of response. This means breaking away from the traditionally heavy style of punctuation which has often been unthinkingly retained as a result of the deplorable but common practice of basing an allegedly 'new' edition on a marked-up copy of an earlier one. Modern practice is so flexible that it is impossible to legislate in ways that would be generally acceptable, but it certainly seems best to be sparing with stops such as the semi-colon, the colon, and the exclamation mark, and editors might valuably look for models rather in current literary and dramatic practice than in academic text-books.

*   *   *

This essay originated in the attempt to define a rational approach to the scholarly problems incurred in modernizing the spelling of words in Shakespeare's text. It seeks to explore the principles applicable to areas in which problems arise, not to offer recommendations in every specific instance. Much must depend upon individual judgement. But as a result of undertaking this investigation, I have come to feel that in some areas the modernizing process could, and should, be taken further than has been customary. Editors who have devoted thought to the matter have been inclined to concern themselves exclusively, or mainly, with the question of whether to accept or reject spellings first adopted by eighteenth-century editors. What is desirable is an examination of far more of the words of each text, in context, with a view to determining their proper modern form. The aim is not simply to make reading easier for those unaccustomed to Elizabethan spelling. Serious consideration of the form that each word should take requires hard thought about the meaning of that word; and the choice of a form, when the possibility of choice exists—and the possibility is not always self-evident—communicates the results of such thought. Editors who undertake this labour may be surprised to find how much that is of interest in Shakespeare's language has gone unnoticed. And our over-all view of the plays may be materially affected. For instance, preliminary work on *As You Like It* suggests that Shakespeare located the action more firmly in France than has been supposed, and than editors' presentation of the text conveys; there is at least a case for spelling 'Ardenne' (not 'Arden'), 'de Bois' (not 'de Boys') and, at some points, for expanding the abbreviation 'Mr' to 'Monsieur'—a word which occurs several times without abbreviation—instead of 'Master', as is traditional. Modernization of spelling, responsibly undertaken, may thus be seen not, as some would have it, as a work of popularization, even of vulgarization, but as a means of exploring Shakespeare's text that can make a real contribution to scholarship.

INDEX OF WORDS DISCUSSED

Words are normally listed under their standard modern spelling

academy, 17
account, 6, 8
against, 9
alarum, 9
alembic, 9
an, 16
apricot, 6, 7, 8, 14
arisen, 7
arose, 7
arrest, 9
astonish, 9

bankrupt, 6, 8
banquet, 6
battered, 22
boil, 6
breese, 15
breeze, 15
buckram, 8
burden, 6

caitiff, 6
candlestick, 9
'cham (= ich am), 13–14
chopine, 5
conceit, 8
corpse, 9
cote, 11
count, 8
courtesy, 10–11
curtsy, 11

debt, 8
debtor, 8
deceit, 8
devil, 27
divers, 12
diverse, 12

-ed *endings*, 26
eisell, eisel, 5
eleven, 13
enough, 13
errand, 6
-est *endings*, 22
eyne, eyen, 7

fallen, 22
far, 26
fastened, 22
fathom, 6
forsaken, 7
forsook, 7
frenzy, 7

hautboy, 15
he, 25
helped, 7
holp, 7
human, 12
humane, 12

ignominy, 9
ingenious, 12
ingenuous, 12
isle, 8

kecksy, 5
knife, 7

lantern, 14, 16
lanthorn, 14, 16
leprous, 25
limb, 7

margin, 6
metal, 11

mettle, 11
mistaken, 7
mistook, 7
more, 12–13, 17
murder, 6

nearer, 26
neither, 23
never, 22–3

oboe, 15
of, 25
on, 25
osprey, 6
ostler, 9

parmacety, 14
peise, 5
porcupine, 7
precedent, 6

quote, 11

rapt, 18
rhyming words, 8, 17

St. Albans, 8

salad, 15–16
samphire, 7
sat, 8
seely, 15
sheriff, 7
sherry, 15
silly, 15
spermaceti, 14
spoke, spake, 7
stolen, 22
struck, 8
subtle, 7, 9
sulphurous, 25
sutler, 5
swoon, 7, 9, 16

tattered, 6
through, 17
travail, 11
travel, 11

venture, 6
vile, 7, 9

whether, 22
wrack, 11–12
wreck, 11–12 ,

Three Studies in the
Text of *Henry V*

INTRODUCTION

Henry V survives in two important texts, the 'bad' Quarto of 1600 and the Folio of 1623. Any edition of the play must be based upon a theory of the nature of these texts, and of the relationship between them. The Folio version is much fuller and more accurate than the Quarto, and shows clear signs of having been printed from Shakespeare's own papers; so all editions of the play have been, and will continue to be, based upon it. The Quarto is nevertheless important, for at least three reasons. First, because it has been claimed that the Folio text was itself printed, in part, from an annotated copy of the first Quarto, or the 1602 or 1619 reprint. Second, because (since all textual transmission introduces error) we have every reason to expect that the Folio text contains errors—some obvious, but some not—which might be corrected by reference to the Quarto. Third, because the Quarto appears to derive from an acting version, and so may contain revisions made by Shakespeare, either in transcribing the foul papers from which the Folio text was later printed, or as a consequence of suggestions made in rehearsal and production.

The three essays which follow explore these possibilities, in the hope of formulating a new and more precise estimate of how much attention editors of the play should give to the Quarto. In the first I have tried to refute the theory—advanced by A. S. Cairncross in 1956, and since endorsed in whole or part by several influential scholars—that the Folio was printed from an annotated copy of a reprint of the Quarto. Consideration of this theory requires detailed bibliographical analysis which will appeal only to the specialist; but this essay is placed first because the question affects the integrity of both our texts of the play. The second essay deals with issues of greater magnitude and more general interest. It attempts to prove that the Quarto is based upon a deliberate adaptation and abridgement of *Henry V*, designed for performance, probably in the provinces, by a cast of eleven. Its conclusions and its methodology have a bearing on Elizabethan theatrical practice, and on theatrical adaptation in general. Specifically, its conclusions support some radical revisions in the accepted text of *Henry V*. The third essay investigates how far the Quarto can be trusted in matters of verbal detail, and attempts to isolate where and how we should look for Quarto readings which may be corrections or authorial revisions of those in the Folio; in the process it tries to formulate principles which are applicable to other plays—such as *Hamlet* and *Dr Faustus*—which survive in reported texts.

QUARTO COPY FOR THE FOLIO TEXT
A REFUTATION

IN 1956 Andrew S. Cairncross advanced the thesis that the Folio text of *Henry V* was printed, in large part, from annotated copies of the second (1602) and third (1619) quartos, a thesis since wholly or partially endorsed by Alice Walker, J. H. Walter, Fredson Bowers, Alfred Harbage, and G. Blakemore Evans.[1] As Cairncross himself observed, the thesis is revolutionary in its editorial implications, for it redefines the relationship and reliability of our two witnesses to the text of the play. Most obviously, it challenges the accuracy and independence of the Folio, the copy-text of every modern edition. But it also, paradoxically, diminishes the importance of the 1600 quarto, by denying its independence. Though some Folio readings, derived from corruptions in Q3, must presumably be replaced by the 'original' Q1 variant, that quarto loses its value as corroborative evidence of Folio readings, and most of its value in correcting Folio errors—for though, according to Cairncross, the agreement of Quarto and Folio proves nothing, where the Folio deliberately departs from the reading of its quarto copy, the quarto copy must presumably be wrong. It should be obvious therefore that editors of *Henry V* cannot afford to ignore the Cairncross hypothesis. And yet they have done so for over twenty years. J. H. Walter in 1960 published an appendix to the revised edition of his new Arden *Henry V* challenging some of Cairncross's evidence, but nevertheless he declared much of it convincing, and implicitly endorsed much else; he did not, however, alter any of his own readings. This can perhaps be forgiven, as a thorough response to Cairncross would have meant re-doing his entire edition. But it is rather more difficult to excuse the nonchalance of subsequent editors, particularly of G. Blakemore Evans, who in his Riverside edition declared that 'some kind of bibliographical link between Q3 . . . and the F1 text seems nearly certain' (972), collated 'the most significant

[1] Cairncross, 'Quarto Copy for Folio *Henry V*', *SB* 8 (1956), 67-93; Walker, 'Some Editorial Principles, with Special Reference to *Henry V*', *SB* 8 (1956), 99 ('Mr. Cairncross's evidence seems to me very strong indeed'), 100; Walter, new Arden *King Henry V* (London, 1954, rev. edn., 1960), 168-73; Bowers, *On Editing Shakespeare* (Charlottesville, 1966), 23, 54, 58, 195; Harbage, *Complete Works* (Baltimore, 1969), 744; Evans, *The Riverside Shakespeare* (Boston, 1974), 972.

agreements between Q3 and F1', and even *added* to Cairncross's evidence of Q3 dependence, but then proceeded to edit the play as though Cairncross had never existed.[1]

In what follows I hope to establish the independence of the Folio text, and thus, in a rather different sense, the independence of the Quarto as well. A few of my arguments have been anticipated by Walter, but because I believe he is himself sometimes mistaken, and also because the entire question needs to be comprehensively re-examined from scratch, I will scrutinize all the evidence on which Cairncross and subsequently Evans based their case, and not simply the evidence 'left over', as unaccounted for, by Walter. I believe it can be convincingly shown that no bibliographical link exists between Q3, or Q2, and F1. What follows then is primarily destructive: it will return us, as it were, to square one. We may lament, with Dr Johnson, the fact that so much criticism consists of demolition; but the demolition must be done, and the fruits are not after all entirely negative. For to tear down an edifice, we must discover, or invent, the proper tools, and those tools are usually relevant to other tasks. *Henry V* is not, of course, the only Folio play alleged to have been set from corrected Quarto copy. But even if we restrict our attention to the future editing of *Henry V* itself, by going backwards we are enabled to go forward, for by establishing the bibliographical independence of Quarto and Folio, we are laying the foundations for a new and reasoned eclecticism, which will be described in the two essays to follow.

*   *   *

Only about half of Cairncross's article is actually devoted to proving the dependence of F on parts of two reprints of Q1; the rest is devoted to an examination of the consequences of that hypo-thesis, of the mechanics of using Q2 and Q3 as copy, and of the motives for doing so. These supplementary speculations of course prove nothing in themselves, being entirely dependent on the conclusion reached elsewhere, that F was printed from corrected exemplars of Q2 and Q3. But the organization of the original article makes it difficult to keep this distinction in mind, for evidence of

---

[1] In fact Evans's own copy-text appears to have been an annotated exemplar of the 1942 Riverside Press edition, edited by W. A. Neilson and C. J. Hill. This is supported by a survey of errors in the Riverside text, particularly those cited in reviews, in Evans's own corrigenda, and in *Henry V* itself.

the alleged bibliographical link is scattered throughout the later and
logically supplementary sections. In what follows, then, I have
included those later arguments (as well as those added by Evans) in
the context of the category of evidence to which they properly
belong.

The evidence for dependence on Q2 is necessarily distinct from
the evidence for dependence on Q3, and can be treated separately.
Cairncross first offers the following verbal parallels, italicizing the
'correct or probably correct' reading (p. 69):

(1)   870   world Q2, F; *word* Q1, 3
(2) 1913   lewer Q1, 2; fewer F; *lower* Q3
(3) 2718   toward Q1, 2, F; *towards* Q3

Of these, the third is of course an absolutely indifferent variant
(Walter, 170). Coincidence of reading does not, in itself, establish
the Folio's dependence on a quarto; it is equally compatible with
the assumption that Q1 is a memorial text derived from some foul-
paper manuscript which served as Folio copy. The Folio's dependence on Q2 and/or Q3 can only be proven by showing that Folio
readings which are clearly wrong derive from a printing error or
variant in these later, and entirely unauthoritative quartos.[1] Cairncross must thus establish two things: that the Folio reading is
wrong, and that it derives from a change made by Q2 from its copy-
text Q1. With a variant *toward/towards*, there is no intrinsic basis for
determining which is right: an editor's decision will depend upon
(rather than determine) his opinion of the copy. I belabour this
point because it is a recurrent logical weakness in Cairncross's case.
As it happens the same variant also illustrates another of his recurrent weaknesses, inaccuracy.[2] He reports that Q1 reads *towards*.
This is not true. If it were true, Cairncross could point to the coincidence between F and the accidental variant of a derivative Quarto—
though even then, he would not have established that F was wrong.
As it is, F, Q1, and Q2 all agree against the derivative Q3.

[1] See the discussion of the distinction between, and relative evidential value of,
indifferent variants and definite errors, in J. K. Walton, *The Quarto Copy for the First
Folio of Shakespeare* (Dublin, 1971), 64.
[2] For his inaccuracy elsewhere, see T. H. Howard-Hill, 'The Compositors of
Shakespeare's Folio Comedies', *SB* 26 (1973), 61–106, and 'Compositors B and E in
the Shakespeare First Folio and Some Recent Studies' (1976, privately circulated
typescript); John O'Connor, 'Compositors D and F of the Shakespeare First Folio',
SB 28 (1975), 81–117; and the review of his *Henry VI* texts by R. K. Turner in *Shakespeare Studies*, 3 (1967), 167–72.

The second variant was also dismissed by Walter (p. 169). The first looks more convincing. But after Cairncross's article and Walter's appendix, Hilda Hulme pointed out that 'world' was listed by *OED* as a legitimate spelling of 'word' from the thirteenth to the sixteenth centuries, and besides this passage, she pointed to another in *As You Like It*, where Shakespeare's manuscript probably read 'world' for 'word'.[1] F's 'world' can thus be added to Dover Wilson's list of unusual spellings which suggest the use of autograph copy.[2] The Q2 reading is either a misprint, or the eruption of a compositor's own spelling. Again, coincidences of this kind prove nothing, so long as they are the reasonable consequence of the operation of entirely independent agents (a foul-paper spelling, a misprint) or the consequence of the same agent operating independently (the spelling 'world' in the personal orthography of Shakespeare and of a Q2 compositor).

Scattered throughout the remainder of the article Cairncross offers a number of other verbal parallels.

(4)   913   busied Q1, 2, F; troubled Q3
(5) 2245   all are Q1, 2, F; are all Q3
(6) 2255   Lord Q1, 2, F; Lords Q3
(7) 2743   in person Q3; Q1, 2, F omit (F: 'which your Maiestie is take out of the Helmet of *Alanson*.')
(8) 2748   in's Q3: in his Q1, 2, F (F: 'with my Gloue in his Cappe')
(9) 2830   O God Q3; God Q1, 2, F (F: 'On one part and on th'other, take it God'; Q3: 'Take it O God, for it is onely thine'.)
(10) 2835   proclaim'd Q3; proclaimed Q1, 2, F (F: 'And be it death proclaymed through our Hoast'; Q3: 'Let it be death proclaim'd to any man'.)

These can be dismissed in one breath: they do not prove that quarto copy was used, but only that, *assuming* the use of quarto copy, it was Q2 (or Q1) rather than Q3. In each case, F and Q1 and Q2 agree

[1] *Explorations in Shakespeare's Language* (London, 1962), 207-8. Two other passages in Shakespeare also witness to the confusion of the two spellings: *Richard II* 3.2.56, where F2 prints 'wordly' for the 'worldly' of all other editions, and *Titus Andronicus* 5.2.65, where Q1 has 'wordlie men', the context clearly requiring 'worldly'. See also Sir John Harington's *Orlando Furioso* 29.4.8, where 'wordly' clearly means 'worldly'. In this case, *wordly* occurs in both the manuscript and the printed text (W. W. Greg, 'An Elizabethan Printer and his Copy' in *Collected Papers*, ed. J. C. Maxwell (Oxford, 1966), 107).

[2] *King Henry V* (Cambridge, 1947), 111. Spellings are of course not the only or the most convincing evidence that the Folio text—or, at least, the Folio additions to Q—derive from foul papers. See W. W. Greg, *The Shakespeare First Folio: Its Bibliographical and Textual History* (Oxford, 1955), 285-6.

against the derivative Pavier Q3. In four of the six cases the motive behind the Q3 change is evident: for examples 8, 9, and 10 it is metrical, for example 5 it is the (probably unconscious) substitution of normal for unusual word order. Example 6 is simply a plurals error, as the context makes quite clear. As for the addition of 'in person' (example 7), it is characteristic of the Q3 compositor who set this page, and who on other occasions interpolated 'then to me', 'my gracious Lord', 'it is enough', 'looke you now', and *He makes Ancient Pistol bite of the Leeke*', not to mention expanding 'God bwy you' to 'And so God be with you', and repeatedly adding single words to the text.[1] These alterations have no claim to authority, and the fact that Q2 agrees with F in omitting them tells us nothing about F (though a great deal about Q3).

As the remaining evidence for the use of Q2 copy is minimal, there is little point in subdividing it into categories, and in any case Walter has already effectively demolished most of it. I will here confine myself to mopping up the few remaining pockets of resistance.

(11) 914 Kingd Q2; King'd F; kingd Q1, 3. (F *always* capitalizes 'King'.)

(12) 915 phantastically Q2, F; fantastically Q1, 3. (The F spelling is unusual. Compositor A set this word or its variants on four other occasions.[2] In all four he spelled 'f-' (once in a justified line). However, on one of the three unjustified occasions he was following the reading of his copy; he never, to our knowledge, departed from the copy spelling, and

---

[1] Evidence for the stints of the Q3 compositors is taken from John F. Andrews, 'The Two Compositors in the Pavier Quartos: Implications for Bibliographical Investigation of the First Folio' (Shakespeare Association of America address, 1973), supplement. Peter W. M. Blayney, who divided the compositors differently, has retracted those assignments, in a letter to *The Library*, V, 30 (1975), 143-5.

[2] Six occasions, if we include passages Hinman attributed to C-or-A: *WT* 2633; *2H4* 1840 (C*) (Q1 fantastically); *TRO* 3912 (Q1 fantastique); *HAM* 3160 (C*); *MAC* 153, 250. My compositor identifications for the Folio are based on Charlton Hinman, *The Printing and Proof-Reading of the First Folio of Shakespeare*, 2 vols. (Oxford, 1964), ii. 514-18, as modified by Hinman himself, in *The Norton Facsimile: The First Folio of Shakespeare* (New York, 1968), xviii; by O'Connor and Howard-Hill, in the articles cited in note 2, p. 43, and Howard-Hill in 'A Reassessment of Compositors B and E in the First Folio Tragedies' (1977, privately circulated typescript). In checking recurrences of a word in the Folio I have used *The Harvard Concordance to Shakespeare*, ed. Marvin Spevack (1973), and then checked each listing in the relevant Oxford Shakespeare Concordance, ed. T. H. Howard-Hill (1969-73), or in a facsimile. Because Spevack's concordance is based upon an edited text, there is some possibility of errors of omission inherent in this procedure. Cairncross, of course, in 1956 had access to none of these important compositor studies or reference tools.

he never elsewhere encountered the word in a play set from foul papers. The evidence cannot define A's preference; it perhaps suggests a tolerance of copy forms, though of course it cannot tell us whether the copy was Q2 or a manuscript.)

(13) 1919　bable Q1, 2, F; babble Q3. F's 'bable' and 'tadle' (earlier in the line) both seem clearly due to justification.

(14) 1930　*Gow.* Q2, F; *Gour.* Q1; *Gower.* Q3. See pp. 65–6.

(15) Cairncross also suggests that F's 'will avouchment' (2753) arose from the following Q2 speech prefix *Soul.* having been corrected to *Will.*, the correction being accidentally incorporated into the dialogue by the compositor (80–2); Walter calls this 'an attractively neat proposal' (173). But 'will avouchment' is a typical Fluellenism, a confusion of noun and verb, as in 'the phrase is a litle variations' (2542), 'shee is turning and inconstant, and mutabilitie, and variation' (1483), 'Gower . . . is good knowledge and literatured in the Warres' (2679). Cairncross ignores the fact that Q2, alone, reads 'avouchments'; and his hypothetical, premeditated reconstruction of the annotated Q2 copy presumes—as do all his other reconstructions—that a printer, preparing the most legible copy possible for his compositors, drew lines all over the page, and made interlinear annotations, rather than using the conventions and symbols of marginal proof correction, which he and his compositors would of course know, and which were created in the interests of precision and economy.[1] Why should the annotator enter '*Will.*' above the crossed-out *Soul.*, when there was room for it, even in Cairncross's reconstruction, at the left, where Cairncross himself placed all the other speech-prefix corrections?

There is then not a single piece of evidence for the use of annotated Q2 as copy for F. But though Walter and Evans both recognized that the case for Q2 was weaker than that for Q3, the consequences for Cairncross's theory of disproving a dependence on Q2 seem not to have been properly understood. In certain respects, by removing Q2 we have made the theory of quarto copy more rather than less attractive, by making it simpler and more economical. We are no longer asked to believe that the Folio compositors were given such a jumble of papers: transcripts, manuscript copy, and loosely pasted, scissored copies of Q3 *and* Q2. We can also dispense with the hypothesis that the corrector first annotated signature C1r of Q3, found it was too messy, then decided to do it over on a copy of Q2 (p. 84)—for surely, though printed copy may have saved labour for compositors, if it entailed so much preparation by

---

[1] Reproductions and discussions of surviving examples of Elizabethan–Jacobean proofing symbols will be found in volume 1 of Peter W. M. Blayney's forthcoming *The Texts of* King Lear *and Their Origins* (Cambridge).

Cairncross's conjectural printing-house corrector, it was not saving Jaggard time or money. We can dispense too with the need to explain Jaggard's happening to possess an exemplar of Q2. He apparently did not possess one in 1619, for normal Elizabethan and Jacobean printing practice was to base reprints upon the latest edition, and if Jaggard had had a copy of Q2, he would presumably not have used Q1 as his copy-text for Q3.

But in other respects the disappearance of Q2 weakens the case for Q3 itself, for it means that there are now six stretches of the Folio text (2.3.42-2.4.74; 4.1.61-103; 4.3.4-33, 73-116; 4.7.161-4.8.35; 4.8.106-5.1.13) where, though quarto copy was available, there is no evidence that it was used. It also means that the annotator must have done all his correcting on a copy of Q3, and this creates, even by Cairncross's admission, some extremely difficult crowding. Finally, the disappearance of Q2 means we can dismiss, as entirely irrelevant, any evidence Cairncross advances to show that Q3, rather than Q2, was used as copy for a particular Folio passage, for this would only be relevant in distinguishing between two sources of copy; it does nothing, in itself, to prove Folio dependence on Q3. In fact, in examining the remaining evidence for quarto copy, we can disregard Q2 entirely, for Q3 was set from Q1;[1] any divergences between Q2 and Q3 are meaningless, except insofar as they illustrate an important methodological fallacy. If two reprints (Q2 and Q3) are set, independently, from a single edition (Q1), the variants are not progressive (Q3 incorporating errors from Q2) but divergent (Q3 and Q2 making different errors—though there may be some overlap, particularly in obvious corrections of Q1). This scattering of error increases the statistical probability that the readings of a fourth text, X, will coincide with the variants in one or the other reprint—even if it is based upon Q1, or upon a manuscript related to Q1. By allowing himself to suppose the use of both Q2 and Q3 as copy for F, Cairncross significantly increased the probability of coincidental agreement, and whatever the pattern of such agreement, it could be rationalized by the 'scissors and paste' expedient, or by declaring that the annotator 'corrected', by reference to manuscript, a reading in his quarto copy. A method that can prove anything, can prove nothing.

*   *   *

[1] B. Nicholson pointed out that Q3 was printed from Q1 in his introduction to the Q1 facsimile published by the New Shakspere Society in 1875.

We can now proceed to an examination of the evidence for the use of Q3 as copy for the Folio, and as this evidence is more extensive, Cairncross has broken it down into categories, the first consisting of verbal links between the two texts. Again, the italicized variant is, according to Cairncross, 'correct or probably correct'. I have followed each item with its context, quoting this in its F form, unless otherwise stated; Q2 readings are not cited.

(1)   538   *honest* Q1; Q3, F omit
             F 'three or four [honest] gentlewomen that liue honestly'

There is nothing intrinsically wrong with F, and the Q1 reading is easily explained as an anticipation.

(2)   806   *ye* Q1; you Q3, F
             F 'Get you therefore hence'

Again, there is nothing intrinsically wrong with F. Even if there were, the coincidence of Q3 and F is easy to explain, for such 'improvements' are common in the Pavier reprints, while this passage in F was set by Compositor B, who elsewhere changed copy *ye* to *you*.[1]

(3)   844   *at* Q1; on Q3, F
             F 'more clothes on his feet'
(4)   862   *hellfire* Q1; hell Q3, F
             F 'said it was a black soul burning in hell'

Both are indifferent. I find 'fire' redundant, as did Greg.[2]

(5)   969   *brother* Q1; brother of Q3, F
             F 'as self-neglecting. / *King.* From our brother of England'

This kind of caesural line is not at all uncommon in Shakespeare; nor, for that matter, are anapaests. Walter pointed out that 'brother of' is used in *Famous Victories*, sig. f3ʳ, and in *King John* 2.1.547 and 3.1.161. He might also have observed that Q1/3 have 'brother of England' at 2997, where metre requires 'brother England', as in F; and that Q3 alters Q1's 'brother' to 'brother of' not only here, but again later in the same scene, at 1009.

---

[1] According to Paul Werstine ('Compositor B of the Shakespeare First Folio', *AEB*, 2 (1978), 241–64), in *MND* 2083, B set 'you' for Q2 'ye', though in reprinting *1H4* he five times set 'ye' for copy 'you'.

[2] *Principles of Emendation in Shakespeare* (British Academy Lecture, 1928), 142.

(6) 1559   *abraided* Q1; vpbraided Q3, F[1]
           F 'vpbraided or abused in disdainful language'

One might prefer 'abraided' as an Elizabethan variant form; *OED* lists it as a sixteenth-century spelling, citing Greene ('That thou dar'st thus abraid me in my land', *Alphonsus* 231). But *OED* also states that this spelling probably arose from phonetic confusion with *abraid* meaning to start or startle. This is just the kind of ambiguity that printers, Jaggard in particular, seem to have wished to avoid. T. H. Howard-Hill has pointed out that 'readers of the press usually try to ensure a comprehensible text, and so on the marked proof-sheet of F1 *Antony and Cleopatra* (p. 352, sig. 2x6^v) the spelling changes *their/there* and *rume/rheume* may be found. The F1 *Lear* (p. 292, sig. 2q6^v) offers another possible example in *holly/holy*.' He goes on to say that the most likely explanation for such spelling changes is that 'the press-corrector was bringing certain spellings into accord with what he imagined the standard usage of the time to be'.[2] This would presumably be as true of reprints as of press-correctors; if anything, more true. And in fact we find the Jaggard Q3 consistently 'normalizing' unusual or ambiguous or old-fashioned Q1 spellings: 'Shure' becomes 'Sure', naught/nought, graunsirs/grandsires, whilest/whilst, Godmorrow/Good morrow (consistently), beating/betting, disgested/digested, wayes/weighes, Iicesickles/Icesickles, lessoned/lessened, heire/aire, anow/enow, Thayle/They'l, Monsire/monsieur (consistently), bace/base (2), yane/yawne, sault/salt, Turkecocke/Turkycocke, God bwy you/ God be with you, lines/loynes, slyte/slight. It is hardly surprising, then, that Q3 altered 'abraided' to 'vpbraided'. As for F itself, two explanations are possible. The first, and most likely, is that Shakespeare's manuscript read 'upbraided' and Compositor A reproduced it. The word, or its variants, appears twenty times in Shakespearian texts, nineteen as 'up-', once (*The Two Noble Kinsmen*) as 'obb-'; 'braid' appears once, in *Pericles*. If Shakespeare's manuscript read 'upbraided', the coincidence of Q3 and F results from the operation of independent agencies; if it read 'abraided', and the compositor normalized the spelling, the coincidence results from the independent operation of the same agency.

---

[1] The original article italicized *vpbraided*; I have assumed this was an error. Cairncross cannot have supposed that agreement of Q3 and F in a correction constituted proof of contamination, and the only ground for choice in the variants is between a common and an unusual (and therefore potentially 'expressive') form.

[2] 'Spelling and the Bibliographer', *The Library*, V, 18 (1963), 15.

(7) 2364   *for* (Hanmer); or Q1, 3, F
             F 'They'le be in fresher Robes, or they will pluck
             The gay new Coats o're the French Souldiers heads'

No modern editor accepts Hanmer's conjecture.

(8) 2372   am Q1; vm Q3, F (='*em*)
             F 'Which if they haue, as I will leaue vm them'

Another instance of Q3 normalizing a perfectly legitimate contemporary spelling.

(9) 2478   *inough* Q1; enow Q3, F
             F 'We are enow yet liuing in the field'

'Enow' is grammatically necessary.

(10) 2621   *Cryspin* Q1; Crispianus Q3, F
             F 'Fought on the day of Crispin Crispianus'

This is intriguing, not least because Cairncross prefers Q1, which is metrically defective, as well as bathetic. But the interest of the variant is twofold: where did Q3 get its emendation, and is that emendation right? If it is wrong, the agreement of Q3 and F strongly supports quarto influence; if it is right, the coincidence tells us nothing about F, but raises several questions about Q3. Two pieces of evidence, unrecorded by Cairncross, suggest that 'Crispianus' might be wrong: in 1528 the Shoemakers' Guild produced a play entitled *Crispin and Crispinianus*; in 1577, Holinshed, in Shakespeare's source, referred to 25 October as 'the feast of Crispine and Crispinian'.[1] But three other pieces of evidence contradict this: the *Oxford Dictionary of English Christian Names* records 'Crispian' as a sixteenth-century personal name, and the form 'Crispianus' was used throughout by Deloney in his tale of Crispianus and Crispine, in *The Gentle Craft*, part I (1597); and 'Crispianus' was the form adopted by William Rowley in *A Shoemaker a Gentleman* (1608), which dramatizes the story of the two brothers.[2] 'Crispinian', if it

---

[1] Alfred Harbage, *Annals of English Drama 975-1700*, rev. S. Schoenbaum (London, 1964), 22; Geoffrey Bullough, ed., *Narrative and Dramatic Sources of Shakespeare*, 8 vols. (London, 1957-75), iv. 392.

[2] '*Crispian* survived as late as 1587 at Gedney, Lincs.': E. G. Withycombe, *The Oxford Dictionary of English Christian Names*, third edition (Oxford, 1977), 76. Though the first extant edition of Deloney's *The Gentle Craft* is dated 1627 (of which only one copy remains), it was entered to Ralph Blore in 1597, and was clearly a source for Dekker's *The Shoemaker's Holiday* (1599). As there were eleven known reprints between 1627 and the end of the century, and as it is well known that 'as more editions were printed a smaller fraction of them survives, and there is a similar

was the normal form, would not fit the metre; neither would 'Crispinianus'; and Shakespeare might have exercised his poetic licence to elide one syllable. But were that the case it becomes even more difficult to explain the Q3 emendation—the emender would first have to supply, from his own brain, the (missing) name, and then to alter that name to suit the metre. Moreover, there is nothing in the metre, or the context, which requires the '-us' suffix, though it is of course permissible; the question again is how Q3 got hold of it. The editor must entertain two possibilities: either Shakespeare wrote 'Crispian', in which case quarto influence seems indisputable; or Shakespeare wrote 'Crispianus', in which case we must assume that this was either a common or the usual form (as the Christian name, Deloney, and Rowley suggest), and that it would have been familiar to someone in Jaggard's shop in 1619, either because the feast was still celebrated (and Henry's speech in 4.3 strongly suggests that it was, at least until 1599), or because the saints themselves were still well known,[1] or because the saints' association with shoemakers persisted, perhaps in local pageants, perhaps even in signs or advertisements (a speculation supported by *OED*'s reference to 'Crispin' as a common noun meaning 'shoemaker', in and after 1640). The plausibility of the latter interpretation is reinforced by another detail, the fact that the Q3 compositor, who set both this line and Henry's Crispin speech in 4.3, did not correct 'Crispin' to 'Crispian' there, though it would have improved the metre. It was only when he saw 'Crispin Crispin', where imperfect metre combines with tautology, that the repetition reminded him that there were *two* shoemakers, thereby prompting his emendation. The man involved is Compositor (B), who is very

decrease in the number of copies surviving from each edition' (Oliver M. Willard, 'The Survival of English books printed before 1640', *The Library*, IV, 23 (1942–3), 173), it seems reasonable to assume that *The Gentle Craft* went through a number of editions between 1597 and 1627. Deloney's popularity could be a factor in the standardizing of 'Crispianus' as the name of the second brother, and in its familiarity in 1619. In Chapter IX Deloney says that the saints' names were 'placed in the Kalendar for a yearly remembrance, which you shall find in the moneth of October, about three daies before the Feast of *Simon* and *Iude*'. The phrase 'you shall find' suggests that the names may have been familiar, at least till the turn of the century, because of their appearance on calendars.

[1] 'An unlikely English tradition claimed that they fled to Faversham during the persecutions and plied their trade at a house on the site of the Swan Inn in Preston Street, visited by English and foreign pilgrims as late as the 17th century. An altar in their honour is in Faversham parish church' (*The Oxford Dictionary of Saints*, by David Hugh Farmer (1978), 93). Rowley's play also suggests that the story would have been familiar.

probably Folio Compositor B. In sum, the evidence suggests to me
that F is right, and Q3 lucky. This variant cannot establish the use
of quarto copy—though, if the use of Q3 were proven on other
grounds, it would have to be reconsidered.

> (11) 2685   *off from his* Q1; from's Q3; from his F
> Q1 'Downe together, I took this gloue off from his helmet'
> Q3 'Downe together, I took this gloue from's helmet'

The Q3 reading is clearly a metrical emendation, and as there is
nothing intrinsically wrong with F, the correspondence would be the
natural consequence of the operation of independent agencies.

> (12) 2912   *Here a* Q1; Heere he Q3, F
> F 'Why heere hee comes'

(Notice that Q3 and F differ on the he/hee spelling, a point
disregarded by Cairncross.) There are actually two variants here, a/
he and here/heere. The first is simply another indifferent variant, the
result of Q3 normalization, and like all the others it proves
nothing.[1] The second deserves our attention only because 'here' was
Compositor A's usual spelling. There are, however, three other
cases in this play where A departed from his preference in unjustified lines: once (2826) agreeing with Q3, twice contradicting it (1603,
2757).

> (13) 2931   *meane time* Q1; in the meane time Q3, F
> F 'I will desire you to liue in the meane time'
> Q3 'But in the meane time, I would desire you / To liue'
> Q1 'meane time, I would / desire you to liue'

Indifferent; the dissimilarity of the contexts does not inspire confidence. Q3's interpolation is of a piece with the others listed above
(p. 45).

> (14) 2976   *Nell* (Capell); Doll Q1, 3, F
> F 'my *Doll* is dead'

There is no reason to doubt that 'Doll' stood in Shakespeare's
manuscript, like the incorrect 'Douer' for 'Hampton' at 1048, or
'Tenth' for 'Ninth' at 224.

To this impressive list G. Blakemore Evans has added, I am sorry
to say (and the reader, I am sure, is sorry to hear), another nine,
which I will treat as summarily as they deserve.

---

[1] Similar sophistications are: a Q1, have Q3 (727, 728); a Q1, of Q3 (1643).

    1608   there is Q1; there's Q3, F
    2245   there is Q1; there's Q3, F
    2486   all is Q1; all's Q3, F
    2514   not Q1; had not Q3, F

The first three are required metrically, and the fourth necessary to
the sense.

    1160   hapence Q1; halfepence Q3, F
    1645   a Q1; of Q3, F

Q3's normalizations, like those listed on page 49, are indifferent,
and prove nothing.

    852   he sed Q1; sed Q3; said F

The Q3 variant can be explained as an accidental omission, or even
a deliberate one, prompted by the need to justify the line, within a
shorter measure than Q1.[1]

Boy. **Yes that he did: and he sed they were diuels incarnat.**   (Q1, B4v)

Boy. **Yes that he did, & sed they were   diuels incarnate.**   (Q3, B4v)

In any case, the variants are again indifferent.

    285   for Q1; Against Q3, F

This is wrong, unless Evans has discovered a press variant in Q3; F
reads 'Against'; Q1–3, 'for'.

    2308   Q1   Shall thinke themselues accurst,
                And hold their manhood cheape,
                While any speake . . .

           Q3   Shall thinke themselues accurst,
                They were not there, when any speakes

           F   Shall thinke themselues accurst they were not here;
                And hold their Manhoods cheape, whiles any speaks

If we accept the hypothesis of Q copy, 'they were not here' derives
solely from Q3, and is without authority, and therefore should be
omitted. But while overlooking this four-word phrase, the 'corrector' added five words omitted by Q3, and altered 'when' to
'whiles'. The compositor then substituted 'here' for 'there'—for if
the phrase derives solely from Q3, it cannot have been in the

---

[1] Reproductions of F are from the copy belonging to the Royal Shakespeare
Theatre (by courtesy of the Governors); of Q1, from Shakespeare Quarto Facsimile 9, ed. W. W. Greg (Oxford, 1956); of Q3, from the Trinity College, Cambridge
copy.

corrector's manuscript, and 'here' must therefore be the misprint of an interpolation (though it happens to make better sense: 'there' suggests someone *outside* the play, looking in). On the other hand, we could suppose that 'They were not there' is just another Q3 interpolation, by Compositor (B), prompted by the context. Evans calls this 'an important reading' (972).

There is thus not a single convincing piece of verbal evidence that F was set from a copy of Q3. It might be felt, however, that though each parallel is susceptible to alternative explanations, surely the presence of so many increases the probability of quarto influence; but the accumulation of bad evidence does not, by some process of alchemy, produce good evidence. The combined efforts of Cairncross and Evans have produced twenty-two verbal parallels (discounting the error on 'against' above) between Q3 and F. *Not a single one* is in Alice Walker's list of fifty-two unanimously rejected Folio readings; indeed, in at least one case Q3 and F are clearly right, against Q1 ('enough/enow'). Cairncross claims that 'The verbal links are as numerous as those indicated by Dr Alice Walker in her arguments for the use of Q copy in other plays' (69). Alice Walker, in the passage referred to, calls for 'at least a dozen obvious common errors'.[1] For *Henry V*, the verbal links are indeed numerous; what is entirely lacking is linked *error*, which is the only proof of derivative copy. As for the number of indifferent parallels, they are a consequence of the nature of Q3, not F. There are, by a rough count, some 280 Q3 departures from Q1 (not counting relineations, or changes in speech prefix spellings). Many of these departures are editorial, designed to improve the metre or the grammar, make sense of nonsense, clarify ambiguity, and normalize spelling. It should not strain our credulity if twenty-two (about 6 per cent) of these happen to be 'right', that is, if they happen to agree with the reading of Shakespeare's manuscript. This percentage becomes even less persuasive if we take into account the fact that Q1 and Q3 are separated by nineteen years and a change of printing house, while Q3 and F were printed three years apart by the same printer, and in places perhaps by the same compositor, in which case we would expect a reasonable number of Q3/F correspondences to derive from the similarity of the printing agent, rather than chance, or the congruence of copy. There is no positive verbal evidence of quarto copy, and this in itself begins to suggest that no such copy was used,

[1] *Textual Problems of the First Folio* (Cambridge, 1953), 1.

for if it was, we would expect *at least* one or two obvious Q3 errors
to survive in F.

The evidence from stage directions need not detain us long.
Cairncross calls this evidence 'particularly valuable' because stage
directions 'differ from the rest of the text in that they are independent of the memorial process of reproduction, and are therefore
most unlikely, in the ordinary course, to agree exactly with those of
a manuscript such as must have been available for F' (70). If stage
directions differ from dialogue in standing outside the direct line of
memorial transmission, they also differ from dialogue in that the
range of possible variation is severely restricted. If you want to tell
your reader that the Boy enters, how many ways are there of saying
this, besides 'Enter the Boy'? If you want to say that Fluellen, who
has just spoken to Pistol, strikes him, how would you phrase it,
except 'He strikes him' or (in the more truncated diction of the
theatre) 'Strikes him'? There is thus a 50/50 chance of coincidence
in any two texts reporting this moment. As it happens, Q and F
choose different alternatives. The placement of the direction, as
Greg noted,[1] is obvious from the dialogue, and can therefore tell us
nothing. We might then suppose that the mere *presence* of the
direction in both texts told us something, since it is discretionary
and could be omitted. But in a similar discretionary direction in 2.1,
the quartos have 'They drawe' twice (564, 598), where the Folio has
it in the form 'Draw' only once (598). We must suppose, on the
hypothesis of Q3 copy, that the corrector deliberately excised this
useful stage direction, just as he excised 'and beates them in' after
'Enter Fluellen' (1136), excised 'to him' from 'Enter . . . Pistol'
(1882), and reduced 'Hostes Quickly, his wife' to 'Quickley' (530).
The expansive treatment of stage directions in other Jaggard
reprints does not make this kind of abbreviation seem very likely.[2]
One of Cairncross's examples is positively misleading (1.2.7), others
are meaningless (4.1.85), others depend on the variants introduced
by Q3, which is quite free in its styling and rewording of stage
directions (1.2.234, 3.2.1, 3.6.1), and one is simply inexplicable
(5.2.1).

None of Cairncross's stage direction parallels involves error in F.
But parallel mislineations do involve error, and for that reason they

---

[2] Consider the treatment of stage directions in Q3 itself, or in the Folio text of
1H4. (The latter is analysed in Alice Walker, 'The Folio Text of *1 Henry IV*', *SB* 6
(1954), 55–7.)

are far more convincing as evidence of bibliographical dependence. But if there were such dependence, we would not expect F consistently to misline Pistol's speeches, which Q treats (correctly) as verse; nor would we expect F to turn all the prose which Q treats (incorrectly) as verse back into prose, without even an occasional error to betray the presence of Q copy. Both these anomalies could be explained by assuming that the corrector wrote 'prose' at the beginning of prose scenes, thus reducing to prose both Nym's prose and Pistol's verse. But this hypothesis creates considerable difficulty in scenes like 4.7; and more generally, since scene divisions are not marked in either text, it would actually entail the corrector's marking where verse resumed; that is, it entails the further consistent marking of copy already very heavily annotated, and it entails the assumption that the compositors, while setting that heavily marked copy, always noticed, and never forgot, the general instructions on lineation which the corrector inserted randomly throughout the Q text. These are of course improbable hypotheses, and it seems altogether likelier that Pistol's speeches are mislined in Folio *Henry V* for the same reason they are mislined in *2 Henry IV* and *The Merry Wives of Windsor*: that is, because Shakespeare himself treated them as prose, ridiculously rhythmical prose, often falling into iambic pentameter units, but as often consisting of alexandrines, half-lines, fragments, and the odd fourteener. What matters is the exaggerated impression of verse, of metrical rant, and this impression can be conveyed—is perhaps best conveyed—without strict adherence to a metrical norm.

Disregarding Pistol's speeches, there are twelve mislineations in F (1024-5, 1046-7, 1083-4, 1285-6, 2079-87, 2138-9, 2152-5, 2368-9, 2381-2, 2756-7, 2825-6, 3063-4). All twelve were set by Compositor A, and six occur in lines absent from Q3. Clearly, there exists another source of mislineation in F, operating independently of Q copy, and associated with a single compositor: Occam's razor bids us beware of adding extraneous explanations, when one sufficient already exists. However, Cairncross explains all six cases for which Q copy existed as a consequence of Q copy. One of these (2825) will be discussed hereafter (p. 69); in another (2756), it is impossible to tell whether verse or prose is intended, and thus one cannot speak with any confidence of *mis*lineation, but only of parallel lineation. This also applies to a third, where F reads

> *Yorke.* My Lord, most humbly on my knee I begge
> The leading of the Vaward.

2381   *King.* Take it, braue *Yorke.*
2382   Now Souldiers march away,
         And how thou pleasest God, dispose the day.   *Exeunt.*

This is perfectly acceptable, and common: 'Take it, braue *Yorke*' is a bridge, completing the preceding line, and commencing the next. Such half-lines have caused editors innumerable headaches, because they can reasonably be treated as a part of either the preceding or the following line. The only thing about this passage which might suggest quarto influence is that Q1 treats 2381–2 as one line, which Q3 divides into two, as in F. But as F is explicable in terms of its own conventions, the real question raised by this passage is 'Why did Q3 depart from its Q1 copy?' A facsimile of the relevant page (E3) of Q1 answers the question (see page 58).

The Q3 compositor set Q1's line 10 as two half-lines simply as part of a general effort to stretch his text and avoid the amateurish spacing of Q1. We confront again the operation of independent agencies: the treatment of bridging half-lines in a dramatic manu-script, and a Jacobean compositor's concern for page layout and design. (The agencies in this case are not entirely unrelated, in that the frequency of such half-lines in printed dramatic texts no doubt suggested to the Pavier compositor its use as the solution to a typographical problem.)

For the three remaining common mislineations, we must take account of certain statistical probabilities. In the first scene of the quarto text, out of 236 lines or portions of lines Q1 has in common with F, it mislines 74—just under a third. This is in one of the best-reported scenes in the play. If Compositor A had mislined *any* passage in this scene, the chances are very good that the result would have coincided, at least partially, with a Q error—for usually an initial mislineation will disturb at least one or two subsequent lines as well. Moreover, in this same scene Q3 re-lines Q1 thirteen times, only four times correctly. If we subtract lines spoken by Exeter, the presumed reporter (who could also have doubled the Governor of Harfleur), the total proportion of mislineations of verse passages in Q3 is staggering, and the fact that three of these coincide (in two cases, only partially) with Folio mislineations hardly constitutes convincing evidence of the use of quarto copy. Its value is even further reduced by the fact that two of the cases involve a particular species of mislineation evident elsewhere in A's stints, where no quarto copy existed: a tendency to make the end of a line and the end of a sentence coincide.

of Henry the fift.

Saue thou thy labour Herauld:
Come thou no more for ranfom, gentle Herauld:
They fhall haue nought I fweare, but thefe my bones:
Which if they haue, as I wil leaue am them,
Will yeeld them litle, tell the Conftable.

Her. I fhall deliuer fo.

Exit Herauld.

Yorke. My gracious Lord, vpon my knee I craue,
The leading of the vaward.

Kin. Take it braue *Yorke.* Come fouldiers lets away:
And as thou pleafeft God, difpofe the day.

Exit.

Enter the foure French Lords.

Ge. O diabello.
Conft. Mor du ma vie.
Or. O what a day is this!
Bur. O Iour dei houre all is gone, all is loft.
Con. We are inough yet liuing in the field,
To fmother vp the Englifh,
If any order might be thought vpon.

Bur. A plague of order, once more to the field,
And he that will not follow *Burban* now,
Let him go home, and with his cap in hand,
Like a bace lene hold the chamber doore,
Why leaft by a flaue no gentler then my dog,
His faireft daughter is contamuracke.

Con. Diforder that hath fpoyld vs, right vs now,
Come we in heapes, weele offer vp our liues,
Vnto thefe Englifh, or elfe die with fame,
Come, come along,
Lets dye with honour, our fhame doth laft too long.

Exit omnes.

E 3   *Enter*

> In motion of no lesse celeritie then that of Thought.
> Suppose, that you haue seene
>
> (1046-7; not in Q)
>
> As send Precepts to the Leuiathan, to come ashore.
> Therefore, you men of Harflew,
>
> (1285-6; not in Q)
>
> Nothing but Oddes with England.
> To that end, as matching to his Youth and Vanitie
>
> (1024-5; Q3 England./)
>
> Who twice a day their wither'd hands hold vp
> Toward Heauen, to pardon blood:
> And I haue built two Chauntries,
>
> (2152-5; Q3 blood,/)

This may be characteristic of A, or of Shakespeare's manuscript; in either case, there is no need to suppose that it derives from the use of quarto copy.

As Alice Walker observed, the appearance in a later text of a palimpsest of the spellings of an earlier text strongly suggests that the later text was printed from the earlier. Cairncross offers three species of spelling evidence for F's dependence on Q3: the presence of peculiar spellings in both texts; the presence in F of spellings usually rejected by the compositor, which coincide with the presumed Q copy; and the similar treatment of what should be random variants in the spelling of unvoiced past participles.

Of these, the peculiar spellings are the least frequent, and the least convincing. According to *OED*, *owze* as a spelling of the word *ooze* appears from the sixteenth to the eighteenth centuries. It seems unusual to us only because it is not the modern spelling. Cairncross remarks that all other Shakespearian plays have *ooze*; but of the word's five occurrences, three are in *The Tempest*, where they reflect Ralph Crane rather than Shakespeare, and the other two were set by Compositor B. Compositor A set the *owse* in *Henry V*, so it could easily be either his own preferred spelling, or the reading of his autograph copy. As for *Louer*, for *Louvre* (1027), the spelling clearly reflects the pun on 'lover' ('Were she the mistress court of mighty Europe'). The line is also spoken by Exeter, generally regarded as one of the reporters behind Q; if so, the spelling '*Louer*' might have been in his part. The spelling *crasing* for *grazing* (2352) is admittedly unique, but Dover Wilson had already pointed out, in his 1947 edition, that Shakespeare meant *crazing* (= 'shattering'), in which case the spelling is not anomalous at all. *Sault* for *salt* is, as Walter observed, a phonetic spelling of Fluellen's Welsh accent. Cairncross also contends that 'Herauld' (2369, 2370) is unusual in F. The passage was set by Compositor A, who encountered this word eight times outside *Henry V*: four times as 'herauld(s)', three times (one justified) as 'herald', and once as 'harrold'.[1] In *Henry V* he set 'herauld' five times, and 'herald' twice (one justified). Of the five 'herauld' spellings, only the two cited by Cairncross could come from Q copy; for two others (2375, 2790) Q copy does not exist, and for the fifth (2789) Q3 reads 'Herald'. It is clear then that 'herauld' is Compositor A's preferred spelling, and has nothing to do with Q3.

Cairncross gives four examples of Compositor A departing from a known preference to follow the spelling of copy.

		Normal A spelling	F *Henry V*	Q *Henry V*
(1)	243	clayme	claim	claim
(2)	302	bene, beene	bin	bin
(3)	177	belieue	beleeue	beleeue
(4)	323	thieues	theeues	theeues
				(p. 75)

In *Henry V* Compositor A set 'claim' four times (one justified), and 'clayme' seven times. Two of the 'claim' spellings occur in lines for which no Q copy exists. As for 'bin', it occurs in a line so crowded that it includes two tildes, even in the Folio, which prefers to avoid them. 'Beleeue' is A's normal spelling. Of thirty occurrences of the word in A stints (even including A* and C*), only once is it spelled 'believe'—*Hamlet* 2.1.38, on a C* page. The spelling 'thieues' never appears in the Folio, and can thus hardly be a 'normal A spelling'.[2]

Past participle spellings are more complicated. To begin with, Cairncross has distorted the evidence. He lists 'steept' as a Q/F agreement, when in fact F spells 'steep'd' and Q3 'steeped'; he also lists 'disgrac'd' (Q3 reads 'disgraced'), 'enforc'd' (F reads 'enforced', the metre requiring trisyllabic pronunciation). These examples point to another, systematic distortion, Cairncross's inclusion of *-ed*, as well as *'d*, endings. Except in prose, the *-ed* spelling is in F consistently used to indicate a syllabic voiced past participle ending. This convention is not applied in prose because rhythm is less

---

[1] Herald: *H5* 1415, 1598, *1H4* 2418, *1H6* 54, *2H6* 1246. Herauld: *H5* 2369, 2370, 2375, 2789, 2790, *JC* 494, *COR* 1063, 1064, 1105. Harrold: *MAC* 207.

[2] Because of Hinman's reattribution of h2ᵛ, 'Theeues' is now in A's stint; but it was not in 1956.

important, but also because the difference between *d* (or *'d*) and *ed* is of some importance to a compositor attempting to justify a line. Therefore, in considering whether the Folio agrees with the Quarto in its treatment of variable past participles, the presence of *-ed* in verse, where it is seldom used unless metrically required, can tell us nothing about the relationship of two texts, if the two texts merely agree on a metrically required reading. The use of *-ed*, rather than *'d* or *-t*, in prose, could be of more value, except that by definition most of the examples will occur in justified lines, where they are subject to mechanical exigencies that distort the evidence. The *-ed* spelling is thus of very little value in establishing textual dependence, and the three examples in Cairncross's second column (Q/F agreement on *-d*, *'d*, *-ed*) must be disregarded—especially since Cairncross, while admitting *-ed* evidence which agrees with his theory, has neglected to mention the vast number of occasions where voiced *-ed* endings in Q verse have been altered to unvoiced endings in F, and vice versa.

Taking these corrections into account, the treatment of unvoiced past participles in Q and F is as follows:

Q, F *-t*	Q, F *-d*, *'d*	Q *-t*, F *'d*, *-ed*	Q *-d*, *-ed*, F *-t*, *'t*
accurst	chac'd	burnt, burned	digd, digt
alewasht/washt	forc'd Q3, F	punisht, punish'd	outfaced, fac't out
astonisht	practis'd	stopt, stop'd	
establisht	wink'd	steept, (in-)steeped	2
matcht Q3		talkt, talk'd	
rackt	4		
toucht		5	
vnfurnisht			
vsurpt			
vanisht			
worshipt			
12			

In sixteen cases Q and F agree, in seven they do not. The five variants in column 3 Cairncross describes as F 'modernization' of its Q copy; this of course begs the question, but it is worth remarking that four of the five were set by Compositor B, who was inclined to modernize copy in just this way.[1] Column 4 is more damaging from

---

[1] Walker, *Textual Problems*, 9. However, this conclusion is based in part on certain highly contentious assumptions about the copy for Folio *Richard III*, *Othello*, *2 Henry IV*, and *Hamlet*.

Cairncross's point of view, as it apparently represents deliberate archaizing of copy. He explains away 'digt' as Welsh pronunciation, but if so, it apparently derives from manuscript—did the corrector check all past participles against his manuscript? As for 'fac't out', Cairncross half-heartedly attributes this to justification, but if the compositor had 'retained' quarto -*d* he could have omitted the apostrophe, which is in F required to exclude the ambiguity of the spelling 'fact'. Of the sixteen Q/F agreements, three clearly have nothing to do with Q, for F spells 'washt' and 'matcht' even where no Q copy exists (1948, 1156), and another three (pickt, vanisht, rackt), since they appear in Exeter's part, could be explained as deriving from the reporter's visual memory of his part. This would reduce column 1 to six unexplained 'coincidences'.

The usefulness of past participle endings as proof of quarto copy was first argued by Alice Walker, in relation to *Othello*, and has since been denied by J. K. Walton. But Walton's refutation depends upon the reasonable supposition that both texts of *Othello* derive, at short remove, from Shakespeare's manuscript, and that consequently the overlap in quarto and Folio practice may stem from that manuscript.[1] This cannot be maintained in our case, because Q1 is a memorial text, and we have no reason to suppose it could reproduce Shakespeare's treatment of such details. J. H. Walter, specifically in reply to Cairncross, dismissed this entire argument by saying that such spellings were arbitrary, 'and therefore a large proportion of agreements between Q and F must be expected' (172). If the spellings were indeed arbitrary, we would have no reason to expect as much agreement as we find; such agreement is explicable only if there is a *pattern* to the treatment of past participles. And in fact such a pattern is clearly discernible in F. In *Henry V* Compositor A consistently uses -t after words ending in -ch. In words ending in -p, Compositor A consistently uses -t, Compositor B always uses 'd (or -ed). In words ending in -sh, A uses -t thirteen times, and 'd only twice; neither of the exceptions derives from Q, and in fact both exceptions occur in words which A elsewhere spelled with -t. In words ending in the phoneme -k (spelled -k or -ck), B uses 'd; A, in nine cases, uses 'd only three times, two of these being in justified lines. A never uses 'd after the spelling -ck. In words ending in the phoneme -s (spelled -s or -c), A uses -t thirteen times, B only once; A uses 'd sixteen times, B six times. The relative compositorial preferences are clear, especially when account is taken of the greater

[1] Walker, *Textual Problems*, 153–6; Walton, 213–15.

length of A's stints in this play. Some very slight weight might be given to departures from that preference, in the direction of Q copy, especially in B's case; but B's one -t (supprest 709) does not occur in Q. A's preference is of course much less reliable, but even so, of his two agreements with Q, 'chas'd' probably derives from a desire to avoid the ambiguity of 'chast'; and A spells 'accurst' on two other occasions (*3 Henry VI* 232, *Richard III* 2551) and 'accurs'd' only once (*The Winter's Tale* 635).[1]

To summarize: the Folio's treatment of unvoiced past participles is not random, but based upon a predictable pattern of compositorial preferences, which has no relation to the existence of quarto copy.

Cairncross also advances three other species of evidence which are closely related to spelling evidence, in that they involve neither error, nor substantive readings, but the presence of a pattern in the accidentals of the Folio text which can only be explained as the half-visible survival of a pattern of such accidentals in the Quarto. Since the Quarto pattern is a result of the decisions and habits of the Quarto compositors, we would not expect it to be reproduced in the Folio, by different compositors with different habits, unless the Folio compositors were setting from Quarto copy, and sometimes simply reproduced the accidentals of that copy, rather than enforcing their own preferences. Cairncross's three types of evidence in this category are punctuation, italics, and speech prefixes.

Punctuation is the least convincing. Several of the examples involve F's peculiar use of colons, and these have already been dismissed by Walter (173). Of the remainder, one involves F's failure to hyphenate 'great grandfather' (of the four other occurrences of this word in the Folio, none is hyphenated). Another involves a comma, common to Q and F, but omitted by the Cambridge editors—those repositories of all textual wisdom—in a line (576: *Doll* / *Teare-sheete*, she by name, and her espouse.) of unusual syntax, where there are three differences in italicization,

---

[1] After -ch: besmyrcht, dispatcht, enricht, fetcht, matcht, smyrcht, toucht, pleach'd, beseech'd (MacMorris's pronunciation of 'besieged'). After -p: A: chopt, vsurpt, whipt, worshipt, hop'd; B: insteeped, steep'd, stop'd. After -sh: ale-washt, crush'd/crusht, dasht, establisht, famisht, flesh'd/flesht, leasht, vanisht (2), punisht, vnfurnisht, vnwisht, washt. After the phoneme -k: B: shak'd, wink'd; A: deckt, enlynckt, pickt, pluckt, wrackt (j), lik'd, rakt, rebuk'd (j), talk'd (j). After the phoneme -s: B: supprest, caus'd, chac'd, enforc'd, forc'd, espous'd, practis'd; A: accurst, addrest, ceast, chanc't, fac't, fixt, glanc't, past (5), plac't, aduis'd, chas'd, compos'd, compris'd, confus'd, defus'd, disgrac'd, dispos'd, enclos'd, farc'd, excus'd, fac'd, promis'd, ros'd, suppos'd.

two in spelling, one in lineation, and another in punctuation, between Q3 and F. The third, 'at least unusual enough to be taken as a clue' (75), involves the combination in F of two practices common enough elsewhere, the placing of a question mark after, rather than before, 'quoth I' (see, for instance, *Richard II* 2658), and the placing of 'quoth I' in parentheses (see, for instance, *3 Henry VI* 2133): the result, '(quoth I?)', though unusual, is an intelligible conflation. Even so, if this were Q's punctuation, the coincidence might indeed be taken as a 'clue'; as Q omits the parentheses, however, there seems no reason to infer Q influence.

Cairncross's argument from italicization, centring on the word 'Dolphin', has been seriously undermined by Hinman's re-attribution of h2^v from B to A; all the word's occurrences now fall within A's stints, and there can be no contrast between the practice of the two compositors. A uses roman type eight times, six of these coinciding with Q3. But since Q3 almost invariably uses roman for the word, any inconsistency in A's practice would automatically *appear* to be the result of Q influence. However, two cases for which no Q copy existed (383, 893) contradict the hypothesis, as does the fact that Compositor A seems in other plays to have preferred roman for the word, setting it in italic only once outside *Henry V* (*1 Henry VI* 2181). Here, though, he seems to prefer italic slightly, using it eleven times—only once agreeing with Q3. In order of printing, A first set six roman, then nine italic, then two roman, then two italic. Indeed, if we revise the setting order of the two pages of the third forme—and Hinman himself[1] admits that there is no conclusive evidence of page order here, and that it would have been natural for A to go straight from h4^v to h5—the pattern is even more striking: seven roman (consistent with A's practice hereto-fore), switching to italic in the course of h2^v, and continuing in italic—with only one exception—to the end of the play. All the evidence suggests compositorial inconsistency, rather than quarto copy.

The evidence of speech prefixes is considerably more complicated. Cairncross first points to several individual anomalies, beginning

[1] Hinman (ii. 17) specifically states that the evidence for the precedence of h2^v and h5 is inconclusive. In fact, the Dolphin evidence is to my mind conclusive as to the order of the two pages. If h2^v was set first, A switched to italic in the middle of column a, used it nine times, and then reverted to roman at the beginning of *the very next page* he set (h5). If however h5 was set first, A's single reversion to his previous roman norm can be explained by the fact that it occurs a full four pages after the nine italics.

with the unique prefix *Pi.* (601), common to Q3 and F but not Q1. A comparison of the three texts immediately explains the coincidence.

Pȷ̃. Sword is an oath, and oathes muſt haue their courſe.   (Q1, B2)

Pȷ.Sword is an oath,and oathes muſt haue their courſe.   (Q3, B2)

Pȷ. Sword is an Oath,& Oaths muſt haue their courſe   (F1, h3)

In the Folio this is a tightly set line, even with the ampersand, and omitting the period. Because he had been using the ligature -st- for Pistol speech prefixes, Compositor B, forced to shorten the prefix, would most naturally have done so by omitting or removing the ligature, thus reducing the prefix from four letters to two; moreover, delicacy would have argued against the form *Pis.* Likewise, although in Q3 the line is a space short of the full measure, the insertion of the ligature would make it too long. Q1 (with a longer measure than Q3) avoided shortening the prefix only by badly crowding the end of the line. Another unique speech prefix anomaly is the change from *Hostes* to *Woman* at 834; but as Walter pointed out, this cannot be attributed to Q copy, as Cairncross asserted, because Q3 reads *Host.* Nor need the change from *Flu.* to *Welch.* (eight times consecutively in 3.2) be attributed to the absence of Q copy. Walter offers it as proof that the international scene was a later addition to the manuscript, but the shift into a generic name is perfectly natural, at the moment when *Irish.* and *Scot.* enter the dialogue, and such shifts can be paralleled in other foul-paper plays.[1]

The evidence of the speech prefixes for Gower and King is of a slightly different and more complicated kind. 'For Gower, A uses the full name, while B prefers *Gow.* Each however, departs from his normal practice once (apart from an exceptional *Gour.* at V. i. 36) . . . A taking his *Gow.* from Q2 at IV. i. 81, and B his *Gower.* from Q3 at IV. vii. 19' (Cairncross, 76). B's anomaly is clearly the result of line-justification, as indicated by the obvious spacing of the line:

Gower. I thinke *Alexander* the Great was borne in   (2543)

It is worth remarking also that B's other exceptional prefix, *Gour.*, cannot be attributed to Q, and that, more generally, though B does prefer shorter prefix forms his work always includes a sprinkling of

---

[1] R. B. McKerrow, in 'A Suggestion Regarding Shakespeare's Manuscripts', *RES*, 11 (1935), 460–1, first pointed out that variations in character names were probably authorial. Some further interesting examples are discussed in Ann Pasternak-Slater, 'Shakespeare's Stage Directions' (unpublished doctoral dissertation, Oxford, 1975), chapter 3.

unexplained longer forms, as T. H. Howard-Hill has shown.[1] As for A, this is the *only* remaining evidence of the use of Q2 as copy, and in itself is obviously insufficient to establish a bibliographical relationship. Though this happens to be the only occasion on which A departs from his *Gower* preference, his practice with other prefixes is hardly consistent enough to warrant much confidence in the evidential value of exceptional forms. For Canterbury, he uses four different prefixes, in no discernible pattern, and without relation to Q preferences; for Exeter, he uses three different forms, none of the four exceptional usages having any relationship to Q; though he prefers *Pist.*, he uses *Pistol* (or *Pistoll*) twice, neither exception coinciding with Q; though he prefers *Dolph.*, he uses *Dolphin* four times, only one coinciding with Q; for Montjoy, he uses three different forms; etc. In the context of such consistent inconsistency, the presence of a single variant which happens to coincide with Q2 or Q3 can have very little significance.

Cairncross's description of the *King* variants is marred by inaccuracies, three of which were pointed out by Walter (171). The chart on page 71 of the original article should read as follows:

	Q1	Q3	F
2612	Kin	Kin	Kin
2617	Kin	Kin	Kin
2620	Kin	Kin	King
2626	Kin	King	Kin
2634	Kin	King	King
2640	Kin	King	Kin
2645	K	King	King
2651	Kin (j)	Kin (j)	Kin
2655	—	—	Kin
2662	K (j)	Kin (j)	Kin (j)
2666	Kin	King	King (j)
2674	Kin	King	King (j)

That is, disregarding the occurrences of the F norm, and justified lines, there are three cases where F *Kin.* coincides with Q3 *Kin.* But we also have three cases where F departs from its norm *against* the preference of Q3, or in the absence of Q3 copy. Moreover, the Folio passage was set by Compositor B, and the Q3 passage by (B), who may very well be the same man; B, whose preference for shorter forms Cairncross himself remarked on, regularly introduces *Kin.*

---

[1] Howard-Hill, 'Compositors B and E . . . and Some Recent Studies', 43–5.

prefixes elsewhere, always *against* the reading of his copy.[1] Finally, this is not even the only occasion where F departs from its norm; Compositor A set *Kin*, (409), where Q3 reads *King*.

The most important evidence of a bibliographical relationship between two texts is the appearance in the second of typographical anomalies deriving from the first, and Cairncross offers two striking anomalies as evidence of F dependence on Q; in both cases, Walter says, 'no alternative explanation seems possible' (171). In 2.1, Nym's interjection 'Pish' (Q3 'Push') is printed, in Q3 and F, in the same line as the last line of the previous speech.

> Good Corporall *Nim* shew the valour of a man,
> And put vp your sword.   *Nim*.Push.   (Q3, B1ᵛ)

> *Bar.* Good Lieutenant, good Corporal offer nothing
> heere.   *Nym.* Pish.   (F1, h3)

Three things are worth remarking. First, F alters the spelling from 'Push' to 'Pish'. Outside this passage Compositor B only encounters the word once, in *Timon of Athens*, and there he spells it 'Push'. Why then should he here depart from the reading of his copy? Secondly, and far more important, 'the last line of the previous speech' is, in F, a completely *different* line from that in Q. Third, and most important, Cairncross's assertion, that this is 'the only example . . . in F' of this typographical phenomenon, is seriously misleading. He ignores the fact that it occurs twice in Q3; the second instance (1565–6), occurring in F in Compositor A's stint—and A was of course likelier than B to follow his copy—is not reproduced in F. More important, although this is the only occasion in *Henry V* where F adopts this anomalous lineation, it does occur in other plays. In twelve plays I have examined it appears ten times.[2] *All but one* of these ten were set by Compositor B; the tenth, set by Compositor A, may or may not have been reproduced from his copy.[3] B used such lineation elsewhere without reference to copy, and so there is nothing unusual about his using it here; moreover, the coincidence is not as incredible as it might seem. For the number of occasions where such lineation *could* happen is quite small: it

[1] Howard-Hill, 'Compositors B and E . . . and Some Recent Studies', 45.

[2] *AYLI* 1458, *KJ* 2078, *2H4* 661, 675, *2H6* 2237, *R3* 704 (A), *COR* 2904, 3240, *TIM* 1691. The other plays I examined were *1H6, H8, JC, MAC, HAM*.

[3] If Q6 was the Folio's copy for this part of *R3* (as Alice Walker assumed), A was here following his copy. J. K. Walton, who argues that F was set throughout from an annotated copy of Q3, does not explain the coincidence.

requires one very short speech, following another very short speech
(or the end of a long speech, the final line occupying only a small
part of the measure), in a line where there is no stage direction for
the right hand margin (*Exit.*). Taking account only of the first two
conditions, there are only six occasions in the whole of *Henry V*
where Compositor B *could* have put one speech on the same line as
another, or the end of another (544, 2538-9, 2576-7, 2675-6,
2940-1, 2955-6). Even this number is probably an exaggeration, for
a compositor will obviously not employ such lineation when,
elsewhere on the page, he gives evidence of trying to stretch his
copy, as he unmistakably does in the second instance (i4ᵛ).

On the same page, there are also unnecessary blank lines after 2458
and 2484. The third opportunity is similarly suspect, in that, besides
resulting in a very crowded line, it is immediately followed by

Gow. Heere comes his Maiefty.

*Alarum. Enter King Harry and Burbon
with prifoners. Flourifh.*

King. I was not angry fince I came to France,

If therefore we dispense with these two examples there are only four
places in *Henry V* where Compositor B could have done what he has
done in 544. The chances of a purely coincidental agreement
between Q and F are thus one-in-four. In themselves, such odds are
of course by no means compelling, as proof of Q influence,
particularly when they are contradicted by the evidence of spelling
(Push/Pish) and the differences in context.

Cairncross's explanation of this anomaly is in fact contradicted
elsewhere in his own article. For Cairncross posits, on pages 82-3,

wholesale transcription by the corrector of this page of Q3. This transcription is required in order to explain F's error 'name' for the correct Q reading 'mare'—a misreading difficult to explain if the compositor had the correct reading staring him in the face. Are we to suppose that the corrector transcribed the typographical anomaly? Even if he did—and of course there is no reason to think so—though a compositor might reproduce such details from printed copy, he is probably not as likely to reproduce them from a manuscript.

The second anomaly is even less convincing.

> Q1   And of all other, but fiue and twentie.
>   O God thy arme was here,
>
> Q3   And of all the other, but fiue and twenty.
>   *King.* O God, thy Arme was heere,
>
> F   But fiue and twentie.
>   O God, thy Arme was heere:

'The F indent in the second line is pointless and exceptional. It is merely a survival of the deletion, in the text of . . . Q3, of the erroneous speech-prefix *King*.' (Cairncross, 71)

There is, however, a second explanation illustrated by the quarto of *King Lear*. This is how it prints the end of the counterfeit letter in scene 2:

> reuenew for euer, and liue the beloued of your brother *Ed-*
> *gar.*
>   Hum, conspiracie, slept till I wakt him . . .

In a passage printed as prose, the Quarto ends the line after a single syllable, and indents the following line, though it is spoken by the same character.[1] This is of course simply a convention (which probably derives from the manuscript) for dealing with letters; it can be seen again, in its more usual form, in Act 4, scene 6 of the same play, where after Edgar reads Oswald's letter, the Quarto again ends the line at the end of the letter, and begins a new line with a speech-prefix *Edg*. The simplest explanation for the error in *Henry V* is that Shakespeare regarded the list of dead as a kind of letter or note, and consequently separated Henry's own words from that letter by beginning and indenting a new line. Compositor A faithfully reproduced the appearance of his copy. Or there may have been a speech-prefix *King* at the head of the line in the manuscript,

---

[1] I am indebted to Peter Blayney for pointing me to this example.

as in the second example above. This hypothesis is not necessary, but it is possible, and as Cairncross and Walter contend that no other explanations exist, the point is perhaps worth pursuing. Again, an identical error appears in the quarto of *Lear* (1448), the text being indented properly, but the speech-prefix omitted, presumably because the compositor simply forgot to reach for the case of italic, or because that case was momentarily in use by another compositor. In the *Lear* example there can be no doubt that the speech-prefix should be restored, and no possibility of contamination from printed copy. If the speech-prefix *King* did stand in Compositor A's copy, it stood there because the list of dead was regarded as a note or 'letter'—whereas in Q3 the speech-prefix is part of a wholesale reorganization of speeches, as a consequence of the contradictions created by Q1's omission of a necessary prefix earlier. We are dealing again with the operation of independent agencies. There is not even genuine agreement here between Q and F, but only an *inferred* agreement, based upon Cairncross's selection of one of a variety of explanations for a typographical oddity in F.

In conclusion, there is no evidence for the use of printed copy for the Folio text of *Henry V*. Moreover and more specifically, there is no evidence for the use of annotated printed copy. As J. K. Walton has pointed out, the hypothesis of annotated quarto copy actually involves the presence of two antecedent stages of transmission—the printed copy itself, and the annotation of that copy—both of which should leave their mark upon the Folio text, in the form of substantive error.[1] For instance, in *King Lear* where all modern editors read 'mysteries' (117), Q has 'mistresse', and F 'miseries'; as Greg remarked, 'the corrector, wishing to alter the . . . word to "misteries", wrote "eries" in the margin, but accidentally drew his pen through the last six, instead of only the last five letters of "mistresse", hence F's reading "miseries"'.[2] Cairncross attempts to provide similar evidence in the second section of his article (78–82). He cites two examples of 'excessive deletion', one being F's omission of the speech prefix *Nym* at 531; this example, besides being by no means certain as an error (as 'miseries' is), is contradicted by his own contention elsewhere that the scene was transcribed, and by the ease with which the error could arise in foul papers, or in the normal course of printing. His second example, the omission of Q's 'well

[1] Walton, 132–3.
[2] *Some Aspects and Problems of London Publishing between 1550 and 1650* (Oxford, 1956), 165.

France farewell' from the second line of Pistol's final speech (2976), presumes that, instead of using normal proof correction symbols, the corrector would have drawn lines and arrows all over his copy. Moreover, Cairncross's belief that the omitted phrase should be reinstated depends on a misreading of the metre. F reads,

> Newes haue I that my *Doll* is dead i'th Spittle of a mala-
> dy of France

Editors since Pope have emended this to

> News have I that my Doll is dead i'th'spital
> Of malady of France,

leaving the half-line uncompleted, and omitting 'a'. Thus four syllables appear to be missing. In fact, the passage should probably read

> News have I that my Doll is dead
> I'th'spital of a malady of France.

The second line is thus a perfect pentameter, without alteration; and though the first line contains only eight syllables, this is well within the rules of Pistol's metric. In any case, to add 'Well France farewell' would turn it into an alexandrine, which is, for Cairncross, equally 'irregular'.

In the absence of any evidence of printed or of annotated copy, there is no need to waste artillery demolishing speculations about why such copy might have been used, and how prepared. Compositors may have had a preference for printed copy—but they must also, surely, have had a preference for uniformity of copy. A manuscript in a single hand throughout (a hand B had already presumably some experience of, in *All's Well That Ends Well*, *The Taming of the Shrew*, and *King John*) would be much easier to deal with than a combination of transcript, manuscript, and very heavily annotated print. Uniform copy would also be much easier to cast off, for setting by formes.[1] Printed copy no doubt saved compositorial labour—but the labour of preparation required in this case would far exceed the anticipated savings. Without overwhelming evidence to the contrary, the thesis that any quarto of *Henry V* was used as copy for the Folio text collapses under the weight of its own improbability.

---

[1] Charlton Hinman, 'Cast-off Copy for the First Folio of Shakespeare', *SQ* 6 (1955), 262.

WE HAPPY FEW
THE 1600 ABRIDGEMENT

THE 1600 Quarto of *Henry V* is a corrupt, memorially reconstructed text of (I believe) a deliberate adaptation of the play,
designed for a cast of eleven. The memorial character of the
text, and its editorial implications, will be examined in the next
essay; but as the extent of memorial corruption can only be
gauged if we know *what* the reporters were trying to reconstruct,
it is necessary that we first find out as much as possible about
the abridged and adapted text. The availability of no more
than eleven actors will of itself explain virtually every major
anomaly in the Quarto's distribution of scenes and characters,
particularly in those features of the text we would not normally
expect to suffer unduly from memorial deficiency; it will account
for, among other things, the omission of 3.1 and of 4.2, the
transposition of scenes 4 and 5 of Act 4, and the omission of
the Chorus. I also hope to show that certain alterations in the
dialogue are the consequences of abridgement, not corruption,
and that the printer's copy for the Quarto text was a memorial
reconstruction based upon a performance of the abridgement itself,
and not a reconstruction of a normal performance of the full text,
subsequently annotated by an adapter (as some have supposed).[1] I
also hope to establish several facts about the play as it was normally
performed by the Chamberlain's Men, and finally, to examine the
editorial consequences—not only for *Henry V*, but also for other
plays of the period—of this hypothesis, and the methodology on
which it is founded.

The procedure for establishing a minimum cast depends upon two
assumptions set out by Sir Walter Greg fifty years ago:[2] that a
character, whenever he appears, must be played by the same actor,
and that an actor between his exit as one character and his entrance
as another must be given sufficient time to change his costume.
('Sufficient time' is a matter of judgement, but in fact disagreements

---

[1] G. I. Duthie, 'The Quarto of Shakespeare's *Henry V*', in *Papers Mainly
Shakespearian*, ed. G. I. Duthie (Edinburgh, 1964), 106-30. Hereafter cited as
Duthie.

[2] *Two Elizabethan Stage Abridgements*: The Battle of Alcazar *and* Orlando
Furioso (Oxford, 1922), 120.

seldom arise.[1]) With these rules in hand, anyone with patience and the capacity to count can determine the smallest number of actors who could have performed a play. Casting decisions will sometimes be arbitrary: for instance, though we can be sure which three actors played the three traitors in the Southampton scene, we have no way of knowing which of the three played which traitor. But, if such details are unknowable, they are also unimportant. So long as we ensure that casting difficulties in later scenes are not caused by arbitrary and avoidable decisions in early ones, the indifference of those decisions need not diminish the inevitability of others.

Act 2, scene 2, as presented in the Quarto, requires six actors: Henry, Exeter, Gloucester, and the three traitors. None can be doubled with any of the five Eastcheap characters, who all reappear at the very beginning of the next scene. All eleven characters in these two scenes speak, so there can be no suspicion that they are ghosts created by the reporter. The Quarto text thus, on the evidence of 2.2 and 2.3, cannot be performed by fewer than eleven actors.

The remainder of the Quarto text can be played by these eleven actors. Scholars have sometimes assumed that characters given no lines are included in the Quarto stage directions by accident. But since eleven actors must have been available, and since the Quarto directions nowhere require more than eleven, there is no reason to assume that *any* stage direction in the Quarto calls for the entrance of characters who do not in fact appear. For instance, the Quarto calls for Clarence in 3.6, though neither the Quarto nor the Folio gives him anything to say. Those who have discussed the Quarto as an abridgement have invariably disregarded such mutes. But

[1] According to David Bradley (*The Ignorant Elizabethan Author and Massinger's 'Believe as you List'* (University of Sydney, 1977), 21), 'Even in late Morality Plays an actor very rarely if ever changes identity under twenty-seven lines of dialogue'. But David Bevington (*From Mankind to Marlowe* (Cambridge, Mass., 1962), 91) points out that a change in *Three Ladies of London* (1581) must take place in 18 lines, and that there are 38 instances in Tudor popular drama of changes executed in 25 lines or less. In *Cambises* an actor must change in only 8 lines; in *Marriage of Wit and Wisdom*, in only 5 lines. As Bevington demonstrates, a great deal depends on the nature of the two roles. William A. Ringler, Jr., in 'The Number of Actors in Shakespeare's Early Plays' (in *The Seventeenth-Century Stage*, ed. G. E. Bentley (Chicago, 1968), 110–34), pointed out that in *The Merchant of Venice* Jessica has only 17 lines to change from her woman's costume in 2.5 to a boy's in 2.6. W. J. Lawrence's chapter on doubling in *Pre-Restoration Stage Studies* (Harvard, 1927) points to a number of obvious theatrical expedients for facilitating rapid changes of character, including '"the reversible cloak", a stage device to whose serviceableness in disguising reference is made in Jonson's *The Devil is an Ass* (1616)' (p. 56).

nothing is saved by disregarding them, for other scenes in the play unequivocally require a minimum of eleven actors, and if eleven are available, Clarence can appear in 3.6, as a part of Henry's army, and we have no reason to suppose he did not. The burden of proof is on those who wish to contend that the Quarto stage directions are wrong—especially where these stage directions follow what is specified or implied in the Folio. When the Quarto stage direction clearly departs from the intention of the Folio, then we are obliged to search for an explanation for the variant, before we dismiss it as mere nonsense. In fact, as will be shown, the explanation almost invariably resides in the size of the cast. This means that the Quarto text, so far as the presence or absence of characters is concerned, accurately reflects the abridgement as performed, and this is what we would expect. For it is infinitely easier to remember what happened on stage, than to remember exactly what was said, and an actor (assuming the reporter was one) is particularly likely to remember who was on or off stage.

Of course, to prove that the Quarto text *could* be performed by eleven actors does not prove that it ever *was* performed by eleven, or that it was specifically adapted for use by eleven. Here we must beware a potential fallacy in the method itself, for the procedure for determining a minimum cast is logical and mathematical, and (if it is to have any validity at all) must strictly adhere to the limits of the possible; whereas the actual casting of a production is historical. The historical casting must of course confine itself *within* the limits of the possible, but it need not be driven *to* those limits. In the absence of surviving documents the only proof that the actual casting ever coincided with the mathematical 'ideal' is the principle of economy: the fact that a single assumption (a maximum of eleven available actors) explains so many otherwise unrelated and un-explained peculiarities of the Quarto text, including the peculiarities of 2.2, where this maximum is first reached. If a twelfth actor had been available, why should the Quarto have omitted one of the English lords? It has two, to the Folio's three. This means that, at scene's end, when Henry says 'Now Lords to *France*', he is addressing only two people. It also means that the three traitors must leave the stage unescorted (*Exit three Lords*). This, though it seems perhaps a bit awkward, is possible: Gloucester or Exeter need only escort them so far as the door. (Even this is not theatrically necessary: if the three are near a door, they may turn and go, heads bowed, and an audience will sense no incongruity.) If we want an attendant to lead them off, we must assume the existence of a twelfth actor, which the remainder of the play gives us no reason to suspect. And if there were such a twelfth actor, there would have been no reason to omit the third English lord, who could have spoken his lines at the beginning of the scene and led the traitors off at the end.

But if only eleven actors were available, why not dispense with one or two of the traitors—as modern producers often do—instead of an English lord, or an attendant? For the simple reason that the meaning of the scene depends upon Henry's entrance, surrounded by three traitors: a detail on which Quarto and Folio agree. Editors and producers who generously supply Henry with a bodyguard of mute attendants, or reduce the three traitors to one, drain the scene of its danger, and allow critics to talk of Henry's secure and cruel 'game' of cat-and-mouse with the traitors. But Henry is a mouse playing with three cats. The Quarto chooses to preserve the sense of danger, and dispense with one of Henry's interchangeable nobles.

A modern theatregoer may nevertheless feel that the Quarto's staging of the Southampton scene is awkward and amateurish, and that to perform the play with a cast of only eleven would entail so much doubling as to put an intolerable strain on an audience's credulity. But when dealing with non-naturalistic staging, and particularly with doubling, we must be guided by the surviving documentary evidence of Elizabethan practice, for our own theatrical experience and expectations are likely to mislead. These expectations have been moulded by at least two fundamental changes in theatrical conditions, one aesthetic, one economic. The aesthetic change is the rise of a naturalism which takes offence at any reminder that actors are actors, not characters; the economic change is that, actors having long ago lost corporate control of their own theatres, they have developed an adversary relationship with management, which has in turn led them to restrict the burdens they are willing to bear—not only for the protection of individual actors, but to ensure that the limited supply of jobs is fairly distributed. In combination, these economic and aesthetic imperatives have ensured that the overwhelming majority of modern plays have a small cast of characters; only heavily subsidized theatres, or films, or companies under the corporate control of actors themselves, have been able to overcome this numerical restriction. The heavily subsidized theatre overcomes it by being able to afford to employ many actors; films, which have become the primary medium for spectacular historical drama, can afford a good many cameo appearances by famous actors, because films reach a market vastly larger and more lucrative than any single theatre could achieve, and because those cameo appearances themselves help to attract that market. The actors' companies overcome restrictions of casting, partly by virtue of state subsidies, partly by eliminating management costs, and (most importantly, from our point of view) by relaxing the self-protective, but now unnecessary, restrictions on their own labour, and thereby permitting their members to double. A company like 7:84 or Joint Stock would have no difficulty performing the Quarto abridgement of *Henry V* with a cast of eleven—though their political predispositions, and the play's jingoist reputation, make it unlikely they would ever choose to do so. What such companies illustrate is the (often largely untapped) versatility of the actor, and the pleasure which that versatility itself occasions, within the conventions of a non-illusionist theatre. These are theatrical possibilities not to be despised, and yet the post-Restoration history of Shakespeare in the theatre has seldom seen fit to encourage them. Indeed, they were beginning to go out of fashion—in London at least, among certain social and intellectual classes—long before the Restoration. The Royal Shakespeare Company or the National Theatre (who between them most influence contemporary notions of Shakespeare's theatricality), because they are heavily subsidized, can afford a certain generosity in casting, but even so—and particularly with the history plays—they, like their eighteenth- and nineteenth-century predecessors, are prone to conflate or omit minor characters, no doubt in the interests of aesthetic as well as fiscal economy. Brecht himself, arch-enemy of the well-made play, does much the same thing in his adaptation of *Edward II*. Curiously, this conflation and compression have often coincided with the provision of vast numbers of supernumeraries, in the form of crowds or armies; in fact, the supernumeraries—which cost relatively little per head, and provide a species of historical realism, being in effect extensions of the set—probably encouraged managers to distinguish the actual dramatic characters from the human fluff by reducing their numbers and increasing their size. But these theatrical expedients have little or nothing to do with the plays as originally envisaged, either by Shakespeare or his first audiences, and until we have reconciled ourselves to the amount of doubling which would have been considered normal for this kind of play in 1599, we cannot hope to judge fairly the theatrical plausibility of the Quarto's abridgement for eleven—which was undoubtedly intended, not for the sophisticates of London, but for provincial audiences, whose tastes and expectations would be by comparison relatively old-fashioned. The fairest modern comparisons are with the 1971 RSC Theatregoround production, or the heavily cut three-act text Macready prepared for Bath and Bristol in December 1834.[1] Judged by such criteria, the abridgement is eminently practicable.

Before proceeding to a detailed analysis of the alterations forced upon the adapter by the size of his cast, I should perhaps explain why I have not provided a cast-chart for the Folio text.[2] The actual casting of the Folio itself is irrelevant, and to an extent indeterminable, for the Folio text derives from an author's manuscript, not a prompt-book or a performance, and consequently we have no way of knowing whether mutes or ghost characters or attendants or armies would have actually appeared on the stage. We also have no reason to believe that the Chamberlain's Men would have been pinched for actors, and the gatherers and stagekeepers were in any case available to fill out a crowd.[3] To prove that the Quarto was abridged for eleven actors we need only establish that the fundamental differences between the Folio and Quarto texts are the inevitable consequence of attempting to perform the play within that numerical limitation.

The Chorus is the first casualty, and one may reasonably suspect that someone looking at the play with an eye to abridgement would have omitted him even before the details of the casting made this decision inevitable. He is, as has often been remarked, dispensable.[4]

[1] The Theatregoround prompt-book is in the Shakespeare Centre Library; Macready's 1834 prompt-book in the Folger (Charles Shattuck, *The Shakespeare Promptbooks* (University of Illinois Press, 1965), 145). I have not seen the latter.

[2] The Folio could be played by thirteen actors, if we assume that the third boy, needed to play Isabel, has been doubling adult roles throughout the play; that the French King in 5.2 has no lords in attendance, though Henry has four (even if we disregard Clarence and Huntington); that the 'Hoast' of 4.3 is a literary fiction; that there was no attendant in 2.2, to lead off the three traitors; and that two actors had to change roles during the excursions between 4.3 and 4.4. None of these assumptions is at all probable. We have no reason to suppose that the Chamberlain's Men normally attempted to perform *Henry V* with only thirteen actors, or that Shakespeare wrote the play with that limitation constantly in mind. Ringler found that the Folio could be acted by 14 men and 2 boys, or 12 men and 4 boys (p. 123); these figures are consonant with his estimate of the requirements of all Shakespeare's pre-1600 plays, except *Titus Andronicus*.

[3] W. W. Greg, *Dramatic Documents from the Elizabethan Playhouse*, 2 vols. (Oxford, 1931), ii. 50 ('Tire-man'), 52 ('Attendants'), 55 ('Gatherers').

[4] There have been efforts to prove that the Choruses are later additions to the play. W. D. Smith, in 'The *Henry V* Choruses in the First Folio' (*Journal of English and Germanic Philology*, 53 (1954), 38–57), sought to prove that the apparent allusion

Because 3.1 had to be omitted, for reasons to be explained in a moment, Chorus could not double with any of the four Eastcheap soldiers, who appear at the very beginning of 3.2; nor could he be doubled with Exeter, or the three French who are present at the end of 2.4. This excludes eight of the available eleven actors. Nor could he be played by Fluellen or Gower, for they appear in 5.1, just after Chorus speaks. It can moreover be easily proven that Gower and Fluellen could not be played by any of the eight actors we have already excluded, for they appear in 3.2 with the Eastcheap characters, and they enter in 3.6 just after the three French have left, and in 4.7 they enter just after Exeter has gone off. This excludes ten of the available eleven. The only remaining actor is the one who plays Clarence, a character present at the end of 1.2 and the end of 4.8, both positions excluding any possibility of doubling with the Chorus. Of course, these problems could be solved by omitting one or two of the Chorus speeches, and retaining the rest. But to omit one or two would be to deprive the others of their structural *raison d'être*. If the casting prevents you from keeping them all, it is best to dispense with them all.[1]

The methods by which I have arrived at this explanation for a long-standing problem, being unfamiliar to the vast majority of my readers, may seem excessively complicated and—by virtue of their

to Essex in the prologue to Act 5 was in fact an allusion to Lord Mountjoy; his arguments have been refuted by R. A. Law, 'The Choruses in *Henry the Fifth*' (*University of Texas Studies in English*, xxxv (1956), 11-21). More recently, though, G. P. Jones, in '*Henry V*: The Chorus and the Audience' (*Shakespeare Survey 31* (1978), 93-104), has argued that the Choruses were specially written for a court performance. His case is built upon a series of assumptions I find exceptionable: that the Chorus's 'special nature demands that special circumstances be found to account for it' (p. 99); that the 'special circumstances' must be external; that a great dramatist will never feel the limitations of his medium, unless he finds himself operating in new and exceptionally cramped conditions; that dramatists will flatter a king, but never flatter their usual audience; that ordinary Elizabethan playgoers would have found the Choruses tedious, though ordinary modern playgoers find them exciting; and that aggressive invocations and defensive excuses are in the theatre contradictory, though in life they go together more often than not. The most convincing refutation of Jones's contentions about the unsuitability of the Choruses for public performance is found in the play's theatrical history, and more particularly in the essay on *Henry V* in Michael Goldman's *Shakespeare and the Energies of Drama* (Princeton, 1972), a work he nowhere mentions.

[1] The Prologue could stand on its own. If it were retained certain lines would have to be altered or omitted: 'wooden O' might not always be appropriate, on a provincial tour (if the abridgement was designed for the provinces—an assumption not yet justified), and the last lines, with their promise of future appearances as

very complexity—implausible. But this complexity is in fact an optical illusion, created by the fact that we must work *backward*, whereas a man casting a play works *forward*. He, beginning with a certain number of actors and a text, modifies that text to meet the demands of that cast, thus producing a second text; we, beginning with two texts of a play, must attempt to ascertain whether the differences between them could be the result of the existence of a hypothetical plotter adapting the play to a hypothetical cast. In order to do this we must perform a number of mathematical operations, each simple and demonstrably proper in itself, but tending in the aggregate to create an impression of specious complexity. Thus, beginning at the beginning of the play, we go forward until we discover the first variants which result in a reduction of the required cast. Assuming that this reduction would not have been made unless it was necessary, we arrive (in 2.2/2.3) at our first estimate of the size of the hypothetical cast (eleven). We then go back to the beginning and proceed through the text of the play, assuming that this original estimate is correct, to see whether that assumption is contradicted—or, if not contradicted, whether it will explain the unexplained differences between our two texts. Thus, when confronted by the Chorus—a character not present in 2.2 or 2.3—we must first ask whether he can be accommodated by a cast of eleven. We do this by subtracting from that number (eleven) the number of other characters either present on-stage when he is on-stage (zero), or present immediately before or immediately after he is on-stage (Nym, Bardolph, Pistol, Boy, Exeter, French King, Dauphin, Constable, Fluellen, Gower, Clarence). But this in itself is not enough, for as yet we have not identified eleven *actors*, but only eleven *roles*, and we must now find out whether any of these roles could be doubled by a single actor. To do this, we again apply the same logical sequence we employed with the Chorus, isolating which actors were available for which roles by a process of

'Chorus', would have to go. This in turn would require writing an alternative ending for the speech, unless we are to imagine something as abruptly ridiculous as

> For 'tis your thoughts that now must deck our Kings,
> Carry them here and there; Iumping o're Times;
> Turning th'accomplishment of many yeeres
> Into an Howre-glasse.   *Exit.*

No doubt the adapter was capable of a line-and-a-half pastiche, but he may simply have felt that, without the other Chorus speeches, the prologue was not worth bothering about. But cast requirements in themselves cannot account for its omission.

elimination, no role being allowed to double with any other role simultaneously on stage. Thus, by a roundabout but rigorous procedure, we determine that all the speeches of the Chorus could not have been retained, *if* the play were to be performed by a cast of eleven. The assumption of a limited cast thus explains another important difference between the two texts, and is thereby rendered that much more probable.

Casting difficulties cannot explain the omission of Act 1, scene 1. That scene has in performances of *Henry V* since the eighteenth century almost always been entirely omitted or severely abridged. The fates of this scene and of the prologue are naturally related, for only the dramatic impetus of the prologue can carry an audience through this very slow opening scene, and it is therefore natural to suppose either that, the adapter having already decided to omit the prologue, the first scene went as a consequence, or that, the adapter having already decided to discard the first scene, the prologue became in some measure superfluous. But this is conjecture; so far as the casting is concerned, neither the prologue nor the first scene creates any difficulties.

The Quarto text of 1.2—its first scene—calls for actors of the following roles: Henry, Exeter, Clarence, two Bishops (one, Ely, is a mute), and at least two French ambassadors (one a mute). One speech is given to a 'Lord', but this could be Clarence, who is otherwise mute. The next scene (2.1) requires five actors: Nym, Bardolph, Pistol, Hostess, and the Boy. However, the Boy enters very late in the scene, and could easily double with a character in 1.2—for instance, Clarence, or the mute Bishop of Ely. Pistol and the Hostess also enter after the scene has started, and they could double with the two French ambassadors, who leave before the end of 1.2. This leaves at least two characters, Bardolph and Nym, who could not, in any circumstances, be doubled with any character in 1.2. The first two scenes can thus be performed by nine actors. (In 1.2 Q also asks for an indeterminate number of '*other Attendants*'. With a cast of eleven, there could be two; one is dispatched, in mid-scene, to fetch the French, and when he returns with them, he and the mute ambassador presumably bring on the 'tun of treasure'.)

After 2.2 the first important evidence of adaptation is in 2.4. In the Folio this scene requires thirteen actors: the five French who enter at the start cannot be doubled with any of the five Eastcheap characters (who exit at the end of the preceding scene), or with

Exeter or his fellow ambassador(s), or with the messenger.[1] The Quarto dispenses with Exeter's mute fellow ambassador(s), altering the text to do so (from Folio's 'Embassadors' and 'them' to Quarto's 'an Embassador' and 'him'), and also omits the messenger. (If a messenger had appeared he would presumably have been noted, especially if one of the reporters was Exeter, as is usually supposed.[2]) These are hardly demanding roles, and one is justified in assuming that if the actors had been available, they would have been used. But if the '*others*' of Q's entrance direction included the Constable (required by the dialogue), and Berri or Bretagne (as called for in F), there would have been no actors left for either the messenger or Exeter's mute companion(s). With a cast of eleven, two of the Folio's parts in this scene must go; and it makes good sense, theatrically, that the available actors should be used to swell the French King's entourage, in this the first appearance of the French court.

But the more important fact about this scene has to do, not with the total number of actors required, but with the actors available to play the five French lords, and especially with those available to play the King and the Dauphin. (Bourbon raises special problems, which are best discussed later.) Exeter and the five Eastcheap characters are out. This leaves five actors to play the five parts, and the five are most easily identified by their roles in 2.2, the scene where we first established the presence of eleven actors. The five are Henry, Gloucester, Cambridge, Scroop, and Grey. The Constable cannot double with Henry or Gloucester, for they appear at the end of 3.6, and he at the beginning of 3.7. This means he must be taken by one of the three traitors—it does not matter which; let us say he doubles Scroop. This leaves us four actors, two of whom must play the Dauphin and the French King: Henry, Gloucester, Cambridge, or Grey.

We must now take what appears to be a detour, but is in fact the shortest distance between two points. Fluellen and Gower make their first appearance in the next scene. They cannot be doubled with the four Eastcheap soldiers, who also appear in that scene, or with Exeter, who leaves the stage (4.6) just as they enter (4.7). This means that Fluellen and Gower can only be doubled by the Hostess,

[1] Nor could they double the Chorus. But the Chorus *could* double the messenger (though he probably did not).

[2] Exeter's partial responsibility for the report was first suggested by Hereward T. Price, *The Text of 'Henry V'* (Newcastle-under-Lyme, 1921), p. 19, and has been accepted by subsequent investigators.

or by one of the same five actors who were available to double the French in 2.4 (Henry, Gloucester, Cambridge, Scroop, Grey). However, it will immediately be seen that Henry and Gloucester, who appear in 3.6, cannot double with Fluellen and Gower, who also appear in that scene. This leaves only four available actors: Hostess, Cambridge, Scroop, Grey. But now we must add another proviso: Fluellen and Gower cannot be taken by the same actors who take the French King, the Dauphin, and the Constable, whose exit from 3.5 is immediately followed by their entry in 3.6. Now, we have already established that the Constable must double one of the three traitors (Scroop). This leaves three actors who could play Fluellen and Gower: the Hostess, Cambridge, or Grey. Whichever two we choose *cannot* double the Dauphin or the French King, and must play one of the two mute French lords.

In fact the choice has to be narrowed even further. This is apparent if, for a moment, we return to 2.2 and ask whether we can determine anything about the antecedent roles of the three actors who play traitors. The three *must* be played by actors who were also present in 1.2, minus Henry and Exeter (themselves present in 2.2). Available are: Ely, Canterbury, two ambassadors, Clarence, two attendants. From these seven must be subtracted any which double with roles in 2.1, for no role in 2.1 can be doubled with any role in 2.2. The Boy can be doubled with anyone in 1.2; Pistol and Hostess could double only the ambassadors conveniently. This leaves four. One must play Gloucester in 2.2; this one cannot be Clarence; let us call him—it makes no difference—one of the two attendants. This leaves us with three roles. Of the three, only Clarence matters. Clarence could be doubled with the Boy,[1] in which case he could *not* be doubled with a traitor. If Clarence does not play one of the traitors, he will not affect our freedom of choice, and Fluellen and Gower can double Scroop and Grey; neither need be doubled with the Hostess. We would not normally expect a boy-actor to take either Gower's or Fluellen's part, and the arrangement might create problems in Act 5, when the Hostess—who must play Alice or Katherine—enters only eleven lines after Fluellen and Gower exit. (Q omits Gower's intervening speech.) However, though the casting

[1] Bradley's inference (p. 30) that boys did not double, even if it were correct for the 1620s, is evidently not correct for the 1590s; as he concedes, it is contradicted by the plots of *Alcazar* and *Tamar Cam*, and by *Mucedorus* (Bevington, p. 78). See also Act 4 of *Sir Thomas More*, where the travelling players who present *The Marriage of Wit and Wisdom* tell More that one boy will play all three female roles.

of a boy as Gower or Fluellen might seem odd, as similar doubling is documented elsewhere[1] it cannot be ruled out here, especially in view of the diminutive stature of most theatrical Fluellens. If Clarence doubles with the Boy, and not with a traitor, then Fluellen and Gower take Cambridge and Grey, and consequently the French King and the Dauphin must be doubled by Henry and Gloucester. But if on the other hand Clarence is not doubled with the Boy, and does double a traitor, since he cannot double the same traitor as the Constable, he must take Cambridge or Grey, and in consequence Fluellen must double with the Hostess.[2] This would save Henry from having to double any speaking role at all, for Gloucester and a traitor would be available to take the French King and the Dauphin. The lead actor would not normally do any doubling.[3] But we are here talking about unusual circumstances, an over-burdened cast, and (possibly) provincial rather than metropolitan practice; and as the Dauphin is the only role of any significance which Henry could double, this possibility cannot be ruled out either.

The reader who has persevered thus far is soon to be rewarded for his pains. Either Fluellen must be played by a boy-actor, or Henry must double the Dauphin,[4] and Gloucester the French King. But which of these alternatives we choose is less important than the fact that we must choose one or the other. For the actors who are available to play the Dauphin in 2.4 and 3.5 are not available to play him in 3.7 and 4.5, and it is for this purely mechanical reason that the Quarto assigns the Dauphin's speeches, in those scenes, to Bourbon. If Fluellen is not played by a boy-actor, the Dauphin must be played by Henry; Henry speaks at the very end of 3.6, Dauphin/Bourbon enters at the very beginning of 3.7. But if on the other hand Fluellen *is* played by a boy-actor, Clarence must double

[1] Dick Jubie doubles the Queen and a Portuguese nobleman in *Alcazar*. In *The Duchess of Malfi* R. Pallant doubled a Doctor, a Court Official, and Cariola, a female attendant—this last is an important role (E. K. Chambers, *The Elizabethan Stage*, 4 vols. (Oxford, 1923), iii. 510). In the revival of *The Wild Goose Chase* given at the Blackfriars in 1631, John Honeyman doubled the parts of Mariana (a courtesan) and the Young Factor (Lawrence, p. 73, n. 1).

[2] Clarence, or the traitor doubled with Clarence, cannot be played by Fluellen or Gower, who appear with Clarence in 3.6. It would be possible to assume that Gower rather than Fluellen doubled with the Hostess, if Gower were not one of the reporters; as it is, the accuracy of his part, and the corruption of hers, rule out any suggestion that their roles were played by one actor.

[3] The leading actor is not required to double in the plots of *2 Seven Deadly Sins*, *Frederick and Basilea*, *The Battle of Alcazar*, or *1 Tamar Cam*.

[4] Henry cannot double the French King, for both appear together in the final scene.

one of the traitors, and then he or Gloucester must double the Dauphin. But neither could double the Dauphin in the later scenes, for they too, like Henry, are present at the end of 3.6. With only eleven actors the character that the Folio calls the Dauphin cannot be played by the same actor in 3.7 and 4.5 as in 2.4 and 3.5; if the lines are spoken by a different actor, they must be spoken by a different character. Hence Bourbon.

Once this decision had been forced upon the adapter by the limits of his cast, another decision followed in its wake. The lines in 3.5 which the Folio assigns to Bretagne the Quarto gives to Bourbon, introducing him and thus preparing the audience for his major role at Agincourt. This makes excellent sense in the context of the Quarto. But in the Folio, Act 4, scene 5 is clearly intended as Bourbon's first appearance: he is there identified by name, given both the longest and the last speech of the scene, and lent prominence by his very unfamiliarity among the French nobles.

To summarize: only two options exist for the casting of the Dauphin in 2.4. Either of these options precludes his appearance in 3.7 or 4.5. If the Dauphin nevertheless appeared in 3.7 and 4.5 in our (hypothetical) abridged text, we would have to conclude that more than eleven actors were available, or—much less likely—that the part was split between two actors. But of course the Dauphin does not appear in those scenes in the (hypothetically) abridged text. This means that at the very least we do not have to abandon our original estimate of a cast of eleven; more important, it means that the assumption of a limited cast has explained yet another important difference between the two texts.

We can now return to the two options for the playing of the Dauphin in 2.4 and 3.5. If the role were taken by Henry, not only would this save Fluellen from being doubled by a boy-actor, it would also explain the Quarto's omission of 3.1. For, having already of necessity omitted the Chorus, the Quarto cannot require an actor to leave the stage as the Dauphin and immediately re-enter as Henry. This is the most economical explanation of the omission, although even on the alternative hypothesis, that Henry did not play the Dauphin, the omission would be almost, if not quite, inevitable. For the preceding scene requires four actors, and the following scene four; this leaves three actors for 3.1, one being Henry, and the other two representing the entire army. However, this difficulty could have been overcome if an adapter had set his mind to it: Exeter could have re-entered with the English (the change of context permitting his reappearance), and the four Eastcheap characters could have been part of the army, either lingering behind while the others charged off, or—less likely—leaving themselves, and then returning. This is not an elegant solution, and it may well have seemed better to omit the scene altogether than to do it badly— especially as it calls for properties (scaling ladders) and actions (scaling a wall) which may not always have been practicable on a (hypothetical) provincial tour.[1] I am inclined to believe that Henry played the Dauphin, both because it seems the more satisfactory solution theatrically (in regard to Fluellen), and because it explains most simply the omission of 3.1.

The Quarto's omission of the Jamy and MacMorris episode in 3.2 cannot be explained as a consequence of casting. Only three rather minor actors were available to play the parts, but there are few English actors who could not, at a pinch, passably imitate a Scots or an Irish accent. It has been suggested that the scene is a later addition to the play, but it seems altogether likelier that it was written in 1599 and either omitted to shorten the play or censored, because of King James's recently expressed irritation at dramatic ridicule of the Scots.[2]

The next scene that concerns us is 3.6, which introduces the character of Montjoy. In this scene Montjoy is on-stage with Henry, Clarence, Gloucester, Gower, and Fluellen; he leaves the stage only four lines before the Constable, Orleans, Bourbon and 'Gebon' (= Rambures) enter. This immediately excludes nine of the available eleven actors. The two remaining are Exeter and Pistol. Exeter is ruled out by 4.3. Pistol is therefore the only actor who can double with Montjoy. The one place in the Folio where this would create a problem—Act 4, scene 4, where Pistol and Le Fer enter only five lines and 'excursions' after Montjoy's exit—has been altered in the Quarto by the transposition of scenes 4 and 5, thus allowing a whole scene for the actor's change of costume. The transposition of these scenes might therefore, like the substitution of Bourbon for

<hr>

[1] The scaling ladders are called for by the (Folio) text; the staging is a matter of dispute. Nevill Coghill (in *The Triple Bond*, ed. Joseph G. Price (London, 1975), 236) has suggested that the ladders are used for 'clambering out of the yard' after the King's oration; Robert J. Fusillo, in 'The Staging of Battle Scenes on the Shakespearean Stage' (unpublished Ph.D. dissertation, University of Birmingham, 1966), 336, 338, contends that the scaling ladders were not used, except 'to show that an assault is in progress'. My own position—that the ladders were used to scale the tiring-house wall—will be defended in my forthcoming edition of the play.

[2] E. K. Chambers, *William Shakespeare: A Study of Facts and Problems*, 2 vols. (Oxford, 1930), i. 238.

the Dauphin, be explained mechanically, as a consequence of the limited cast.

The '*others*' of Folio 3.7 have been omitted in the Quarto: the presence of six named characters on-stage at the end of the preceding scene, and four on-stage at the beginning of this, leaves only one available, and he was apparently used, for what he was worth, to swell Henry's army in the preceding scene. (Q speaks of '*King*, Clarence, Gloster *and others*'.) However, this omission has also the warrant of theatrical tradition, for the '*others*' of 3.7 are ghost characters, easily and perhaps best disregarded: even managers with many more than eleven actors might reasonably feel that extras were better spent in the form of Henry's 'poor soldiers', than as meaningless French. As for the four French, the Constable has already been assigned an actor; for the other three, because of the juxtaposition with 3.6 only four actors are available—Nym, Bardolph, Exeter, and the Hostess. But Exeter presents problems, in that he would have to exit at the end of 4.3 and re-enter at the beginning of the next scene (4.5) as a Frenchman. After 4.3 the Folio calls for '*excursions*', and as these represent the Battle of Agincourt we could reasonably speculate that they were also present in the adaptation, though the Quarto does not mention them. However, it seems best to avoid the necessity for Exeter's difficult change, if we can do so, especially since the Hostess could without improbability be given the small part of 'Gebon' (= Rambures). The very poor reporting of the French scenes also works against the assignment to Exeter, whose scenes and speeches elsewhere in the Quarto are among the most accurate portions of the text. If Bardolph, Nym, and the Hostess are Orleans, Bourbon, and Rambures, this means that Exeter had to be the actor who supplied the '*others*' of 3.6. This in turn could well be part of the explanation for the Quarto's omission of Henry's final speech in 3.3, where he orders Exeter to stay behind at Harfleur, a speech which might have been awkward if Exeter was required for casting reasons in the very next English scene. (This explanation for the omission may have combined with another, if Exeter doubled the Governor of Harfleur—one of the few parts he can double.)

The last paragraph contains a rather dangerous assertion, that in 3.4 the stage direction's '*others*' is mistakenly plural, and refers to Exeter alone. I call the assertion dangerous because the reasoning behind it is circular. 'When the Quarto stage directions confirm my theory of a minimum cast, they are accurate; when they contradict that theory, they are corrupt.' This is the brand of circularity which invalidates Greg's entire discussion of *The Battle of Alcazar*. (See Appendix C.) In fact, this single word *others* is the only occasion where my hypothesis creates such difficulty, but as a single piece of negative evidence is sufficient to demolish the entire edifice, it cannot be passed over in silence. Quite simply, all the evidence for the accuracy of the abridgement hypothesis must be weighed against all the evidence for the accuracy of this word *others*. All the abridgement evidence has not yet been presented, but the evidence on *others* can be simply stated. The 1600 Quarto is a memorial text; this was established by P. A. Daniel a century ago,[1] and has been confirmed by subsequent investigators, on the basis of textual evidence entirely unrelated to questions of casting. Since it is a memorial text, only limited confidence can be placed in its verbal accuracy, and though we have reason to expect that stage directions will generally be more accurate than dialogue, we have no reason to expect them to be perfect. In this specific instance, moreover, it is easy to see how the error arose, as the result of a misimpression, the sense that the stage is full: one might easily estimate that there were 'a couple of others' on-stage, when in fact a strict count would reveal only one. Finally, it is possible that there actually were several '*others*', for even a company with only eleven actors might require stage hand(s)—a prompter, at the least— musician(s), and gatherer(s), who could have been used to swell Henry's army here and in 4.3.[2] Consequently, I do not think this stage direction seriously vitiates the abridgement evidence. Let the reader judge.

Act 4, scene 1 presents no problems from the viewpoint of casting, but considerable difficulty as regards the nature of the Quarto text. These problems centre on Erpingham. Though Erpingham's mute presence in 4.3 would require a twelfth actor, he could easily have been accommodated in this scene. But his first appearance, and the section of the scene up to Pistol's entrance (lines 1–35), has been

[1] *Henry V: Parallel Texts of the First Quarto (1600) and First Folio (1623) Editions*, ed. B. R. Nicholson, with an introduction by P. A. Daniel (London, New Shakspere Society, 1877).

[2] Indeed, before the advent of Equity, companies on tour were probably willing enough to draft members of the audience to fill up such mute places—an expedient which has a certain public-relations utility not to be despised, especially for men who 'were never more uncertain in their lives; now up and now down, they know not when to play, where to play, nor what to play. Not when to play for fearful fools, where to play for Puritan fools, nor what to play for critical fools' (Thomas Middleton, *A Mad World, My Masters* 5.1.29–33).

cut, though the actors were available, and though the omission
removes the explanation for Henry's disguise. In the Folio text the
Chorus describes Henry publicly visiting his troops on the eve of
the battle; then, in the following dialogue, Henry borrows Erpingham's cloak, dismisses his nobles, and explains 'I and my Bosome
must debate a while, / And then I would no other company.' Henry
wants to be alone; this is the only explanation Shakespeare offers
for the disguise. But on to this solitude Pistol, and then the other
soldiers, intrude, and it is not until scene's end that we are given the
soliloquy and prayer implicitly promised us by Henry's desire to be
alone. In the Folio Henry's visit to his soldiers in disguise is
inadvertent and unintended, the scene depending on its contrast
with the effect of the populist morale-building walk described by the
Chorus. Henry in this scene makes no attempt to cheer his soldiers.
He deliberately picks a fight with Pistol, even going to the length of
claiming Fluellen as a kinsman; he makes no attempt to contact
Fluellen and Gower; when the three soldiers ask his opinion of their
chances, he likens the army to 'men wrackt vpon a Sand, that looke
to be washt off the next Tyde' (ll. 1948–9), attributing this opinion
to Erpingham, who was in fact full of good cheer. It is only when
they mention the king that Henry enters the conversation in earnest,
defensively, and even then the argument revolves around *dying* in
the king's company, and whether the king should be held responsible for their *deaths*, and whether in the coming battle the king will
die or let himself be taken captive. After the soldiers leave, Henry
launches into a long and bitter soliloquy on the agony of his own
condition, disregarding the fate of the army. Only afterwards, when
Erpingham has reminded him of his waiting nobles, does he pray for
his men, and for victory. The Quarto, by omission and alteration,
has radically changed the nature of this scene. To begin with, for
reasons of casting the contrast provided by the Chorus has been
omitted. Then, by the omission of the opening of the scene, Henry's
personal motive for the disguise has been removed. In the absence of
this background, Henry's unexplained appearance '*disguised*' will
suggest no more than the popular folklore motif of the disguised
king, an Elizabethan dramatic cliché brilliantly analysed by Anne
Barton.[1] The rest of the scene has been altered accordingly. In the
dialogue with Pistol, the Quarto interpolates, in five of Henry's nine
speeches, the word 'sir'. Of course, this throws a very heavy comic

[1] 'The King Disguised: Shakespeare's *Henry V* and the Comical History', in *The Triple Bond*, 92–117.

emphasis on the discrepancy between Henry's true and assumed status. The Quarto also omits—accidentally or deliberately, it is impossible to tell, though these are the *only* lines of this dialogue omitted by Q—the crucial exchange about Fluellen:

> *Pistol.* Tell him Ile knock his Leeke about his Pate vpon
> S. *Dauies* day.
> *King.* Doe not you weare your Dagger in your Cappe that day,
> least he knock that about yours.   (1901-4)

In the Folio it is only after this exchange that Pistol deduces Fluellen is Henry's friend. The Quarto, by omitting these two speeches, gives an entirely different impression: Henry inadvertently admits to being Fluellen's kinsman and friend *before* he has any knowledge of the quarrel between Fluellen and Pistol (of which the audience is well aware). This change again throws the scene's emphasis on the traditional comedy of discrepant awareness, rather than the unique drama of Henry's relationship with his army.

   The Quarto's intervention in the scene with Court, Bates, and Williams is the most extensive literary adaptation in the entire text. The Folio reads:

> *Williams.* . . . Who goes there?
> *King.* A Friend.
> *Williams.* Vnder what Captaine serue you?
> *King.* Vnder Sir *Iohn Erpingham.*
> *Williams.* A good old Commander, and a most kinde
> Gentleman: I pray you, what thinkes he of our estate?
> *King.* Euen as men wrackt vpon a Sand, that looke to
> be washt off the next Tyde.
> *Bates.* He hath not told his thought to the King?
> *King.* No: nor it is not meet he should . . .   (1941-51)

The Quarto substitutes:

> *Kin.* Now masters god morrow, what cheare?
> 3.S. Ifaith small cheer some of vs is like to haue,
> Ere this day ende.
> *Kin.* Why fear nothing man, the king is frolike.
> 2.S. I he may be, for he hath no such cause as we
> *Kin.* Nay say not so . . .   (D4, 18-23)

There can of course be no suspicion that this change results from limitations of cast; nor can it be dismissed as memorial corruption, for though the Quarto in this vicinity sometimes resorts to paraphrase, in every instance but this its text can be unambiguously related to something which does actually stand in the Folio. There are three crucial alterations in the Quarto version. First, the Quarto makes it clear that Henry voluntarily approaches the soldiers, whereas in the Folio it is they who first speak to him. Second, the Quarto replaces Henry's gloomy description of men wrecked upon a sand with the self-evident morale-building of 'what cheare?' and 'Why fear nothing man, the king is frolike'. Third, all mention of Erpingham has been excised. This last fact makes it virtually certain that Erpingham was deliberately removed, and that the omission of his earlier entrance cannot be explained as a slip by the reporter. (See also pp. 143–4.)

The Quarto next omits Henry's soliloquy on ceremony. This is an understandable omission of a very long speech. But again, it radically alters our final perspective on the dialogue between Henry and his three soldiers.

> *Kin.* Tis no treason to cut French crownes,
> For to morrow the king himselfe wil be a clipper.   (E1, 17–18)

In the Quarto this is the end of the episode: good-natured Henry joking with his men, as they walk away. But the Folio immediately follows this by Henry's bitter repetition of their 'Upon the King', so that the preceding banter seems a deliberate falsehood, a role consciously adopted.

What was the impetus behind this series of alterations? We might presume it began with the unavoidable omission of the Chorus, combined perhaps with the voluntary but understandable decision to omit Henry's long introspective soliloquy. Once this latter decision has been made, Erpingham's second appearance (providing the transition from soliloquy to prayer) becomes superfluous. Erpingham's mute third appearance would also have to go, for casting reasons. At this point it may have occurred to the adapter to get rid of the character altogether. But he need not have done so, and even if he had dispensed with him, he could have retained the scene's opening dialogue, redistributing Erpingham's lines to another character. It seems likely then that the omission of that dialogue had to do not with Erpingham, but with the dialogue's content; that the entire scene, as written, had already been seriously weakened by the omission of the Chorus (and Henry's soliloquy?); and that, in these circumstances, and for the audience envisaged, it was thought best to adopt a simpler and more conventional account of Henry's disguise. To suppose that all of these interrelated and consistent alterations, confined to a single scene, are the results of chance, the freaks of memory, is to substitute a dozen coincidences for a single explicable and coherent motive.

From the standpoint of casting, the preceding discussion was a digression, for 4.1 creates no problems for eleven actors. But the following scene, 4.2, was omitted from the Quarto for casting reasons. The new character, Grandpré, himself creates no problems, but if the scene is retained, none of the French lords can double with any of the English lords who appear at the beginning of 4.3. Warwick, who first appears in that scene, cannot double with Henry, Exeter, Clarence, Montjoy, Gloucester (4.3), Fluellen, Gower, or Williams (4.8). This is eight exclusions. If to these we add the four French lords—as we must if 4.2 is included—we are left with twelve actors who could *not* play Warwick, in which case Warwick requires a thirteenth actor. (In fact, if there were twelve actors, this would alter the doubling pattern throughout the play, and 4.2 could be included—see Appendix B.) But if we omit 4.2, as Q does, then Warwick can double with one of the French lords, and the play can be performed by eleven actors.

The doubling of Warwick and a French lord—Bourbon, for instance—apparently creates a problem, though, between Warwick's exit at the end of 4.3 and Bourbon's immediate entrance at the beginning of the transposed 4.5. However, the Folio, after 4.3, calls for excursions. The Quarto does not mention these, but this is probably accidental—*The True Tragedie*, for instance, neglects to mention three excursions called for in the Folio text of *3 Henry VI*—and these *Henry V* excursions are, in fact, the dramatization of the battle of Agincourt, the climax to which the whole play drives. (*The Famous Victories of Henry the Fift* at this point has the simple stage direction, *The Battell*, which thus takes place, in its entirety, between scenes.) If off-stage alarums and on-stage fighting intervened between 4.3 and 4.5, Warwick would have time to effect the transformation to Bourbon.[1]

The perspicacious reader may recall though that earlier the only reason I gave for the transposition of 4.4 and 4.5 was that it would prevent the actor playing Montjoy from having to change into

---

[1] On the possible duration of excursions, see Fusillo, pp. 398–409. A stage direction from *The Tide Tarrieth No Man* cited by Bevington (p. 96) is also relevant: Courage the Vice and Hurtful Help 'fighteth to prolong the time, while Wantonnesse maketh her ready' (l. 1215).

Pistol in the interval between 4.3 and 4.4. If this were the case, the adapter has achieved nothing, for by sparing Pistol-Montjoy he has burdened Warwick-Bourbon. In fact, he has achieved less than nothing, for Montjoy leaves the stage five lines before Warwick. But we are now in a better position to understand the true extent of the adapter's dilemma. Clarence doubles with the Boy.[1] But Clarence appears at the end of 4.3, and the Boy at the beginning of 4.4; if the scenes remain in their Folio order, Clarence-Boy (as well as Pistol-Montjoy) must change in the interval. If an adapter must resort to this species of quick-change, he will surely try to minimize the number of actors involved—especially if one is a boy and especially if he needs actors for excursions in the interim. Nevertheless, it should be made clear that the strength of our earlier explanation for the transposition of these two scenes has been considerably weakened, and we should consider alternatives.

The transposition can certainly be defended on purely aesthetic grounds. It locates Pistol's martial success in the context of a French rout. It also radically alters the impact of the scene, for in the Folio the comic business with Le Fer comes as the anomalous climax to the long structural and emotional build-up to Agincourt. Literary critics may appreciate the irony of this anticlimax, but in fact it seldom works theatrically. In the eighteenth century it was 'usually performed', according to Francis Gentleman, though he remarked that it serves 'no purpose but to destroy the dignity of expectation'. In fact, before Kemble's 1789 production, Le Fer (and so presumably this scene) appeared in only twenty-eight of the ninety-nine performances of *Henry V*, and even these appearances are heavily concentrated in two periods, 1744–6 and 1762–8.[2] After Kemble,

---

[1] Earlier in the play (2.4), when we first considered the Clarence-Boy identification, there seemed some room for choice, but by this point the alternative has become all but impossible. If Clarence does not double the Boy, he must probably double Le Fer, which creates just as much difficulty for the Folio order. If he does not double Le Fer, the Hostess has to; but she must also double York, an arrangement just as unsatisfactory. Moreover, besides requiring the Hostess to double Fluellen, this arrangement would also force the Boy to double Gebon—which creates difficulty whatever the order of scenes 4 and 5. Thus, to double Clarence with the Boy creates the fewest difficulties in Act 4, and seems also most consonant with the presumed physical characteristics and talents of the three actors affected.

[2] Gentleman's comment appears in John Bell's edition of Shakespeare (London, 1774), iv. 260. Figures for eighteenth-century performances are from C. B. Hogan, *Shakespeare on the London Stage 1701–1800*, 2 vols. (Oxford, 1952–7), i. 194–202; ii. 277–94. I have counted Holtom's first appearance as Le Fer in 1762, though in fact it occurred on 29 December 1761—the only 1761 performance (out of 21) which included Le Fer. From 1744–6 Le Fer was played by Destrade; for 1762–70 by

the scene disappeared altogether, until Calvert's 1872 production. Calvert severely pruned the scene, and followed it with a tableau of the Battle of Agincourt; indeed, it was probably only included as a fore-stage scene to fill the time needed to set up the tableau. Even modern productions often insert the last six lines of the Act 4 Chorus, thus providing an imaginative peak to cap 4.3, and as it were 'explaining' the anticlimax in advance.[1] These are all theatrical attempts to deal with the structural awkwardness of 4.4 as it stands, and it would not be surprising if the Quarto's transposition were motivated by similar considerations, in which case it might easily antedate the adaptation. If it did, it would have further advantages, for it harmonizes well with other aspects of the Folio text.[2]

Before leaving this scene entirely, we must at least consider two other solutions to the difficulties created by Warwick. In the first place, one might postulate a break in the performance. The end of 4.3 seems an unlikely place to put one, but it could be defended, and in any case we know so little about act-breaks in Elizabethan theatres—and what little we know is interpreted so variously—that one can have little confidence in arguments from theatrical probability.[3] In fact, you can, if you choose, imagine an interval at any

Holtom. In each case the actor's association with the role probably helped keep it in the repertoire: these two actors account for all but four of the performances of 4.4 before 1872. Moreover, the 1762 performances seriously unbalance the statistical picture, for the large number of performances of that production was a consequence of its including a coronation procession, modelled on that of George III and Queen Charlotte.

[1] The texts of Kemble (1811), Macready (1834), Kean (1859), Calvert (Manchester, 1872), Payne (Stratford, 1937), Quayle (Stratford, 1951), Barton-Hall (Stratford, 1964), and Olivier (1944) are described in the appendices to David Nancarrow's 'Stage History of William Shakespeare's *King Henry the Fifth*' (unpublished Ph.D. dissertation, University of Birmingham, 1975). For modern productions I have also consulted the prompt-books at the Shakespeare Centre Library, Stratford-upon-Avon. Modern productions occasionally omit or transpose 4.4: in 1966, at Stratford, it was played after 4.6.

[2] Q omits the Boy's final speech in 4.4. But if the two scenes were ever transposed in a text which included it, when he says 'the French might have a good pray of vs', the audience would already know of the upcoming French counter-attack, led by Bourbon; this would increase the sense of danger, and make Fluellen's 'Kill the poys and the luggage' immediately comprehensible, and indeed inevitable. See also pp. 150-1.

[3] The most persuasive modern defence of the act-pause is G. K. Hunter's 'Were there act-pauses on Shakespeare's stage?' in *English Renaissance Drama*, eds. Henning, Kimbrough, Knowles (1976). However, as *Henry V* is itself the play most often cited as evidence of such five-act structure, it should be observed that in the Folio text the Chorus speeches themselves fill the pauses between acts, and that the emotional structure of the play would be seriously weakened if a break in

point where the casting creates difficulties. Of course, to do so complicates our methodology, but one cannot dismiss the possibility simply because of its methodological inconvenience. One can observe, however, that in existing plots, and in manuscripts like *Believe As You List*, which preserve casting instructions, in no case do the mechanics of the casting depend upon the presumption of a theatrical interval; and one can also observe that, for a text so abbreviated as this of *Henry V*, no interval is really required. To assume its existence, merely in order to ease our own task, seems an undesirable licence; but it seems equally undesirable to deny the possibility altogether.

The second possibility is that, confronted with such difficulties, the adapter may simply have resorted to cheating, i.e. to having one character played by two different actors. This happens in *Believe As You List*. But it can never have been a very happy expedient, theatrically; and, when dealing with peripheral and indistinguishable characters like the English nobles in this play, it would be easy enough, if one were forced to split one part between two actors, to call the two halves by different names. As the Quarto does not do this, I see no reason to infer any such licence here; but again, it would be undesirable to ignore or deny the validity of this expedient, in certain circumstances.

In the Folio Salisbury enters at the beginning of 4.3, leaves, then re-enters after Henry's Crispin speech, with the news that 'The French are brauely in their battailes set'. In the Quarto Salisbury enters, leaves, but does not return, his message being delivered by Gloucester (who has not left the stage). This is slightly awkward, but it means that the actor playing Salisbury has the opportunity to change into another role. Salisbury could double York or Le Fer, but it seems most probable that his very small part was taken by Bardolph-Orleans, which would preclude either of these identifications. York creates a minor problem in that the Quarto does not give him an entrance, but it seems reasonable to assume that he enters, as he does in the Folio, immediately before he speaks. In either case, York can be doubled by Fluellen, who might also have doubled Le Fer— unless the latter were taken by Gloucester, a very real possibility, although it precludes Gloucester's appearance as one of Henry's

performance preceded each of them. (See my 'To Analyze Delight: Emotion and Response in Four of Shakespeare's Plays' (doctoral dissertation submitted to University of Cambridge), 119-20.)

nobles in 4.6.[1] Given the transposition of 4.4 and 4.5, Le Fer might also logically and easily be taken by Rambures (= Gebon), or even Orleans, who could exit into battle at the end of 4.5 and immediately return at the beginning of 4.4: a perfectly acceptable procedure, so long as a character enters in different company than he departed in.[2]

In 4.7 Q calls for '*King and the Lords*', but it omits speeches by Exeter and Gloucester, reassigns another speech of Exeter's to Fluellen, and alters Henry's final speech to remove specific mention of Exeter, Gloucester, and Warwick. This is odd, because all three actors are apparently available, and the scene self-evidently requires two or more lords to enter with Henry, and to leave at his behest. There are six actors available in this scene to play English lords: Exeter, Clarence, Hostess-Gebon, Bourbon-Warwick, Orleans, and Gloucester. Four of these normally play English lords anyway, and three (Exeter, Warwick, and Clarence) appear later in the next scene, to break up the fight. One hesitates to ascribe the conjunction of all these details to chance[3]—especially as Exeter, the presumed reporter, is probably on-stage himself—but no mechanical explanation is evident, unless we assume that the adaptation included the French prisoners called for in the Folio. If Bourbon, Orleans, the Constable, and Rambures were needed as prisoners, this would exclude all the English lords but Exeter, Clarence, and Gloucester;

[1] Gower is available to double Le Fer, but the poor reporting of the scene—in contrast to Gower's own part, and the parts he *had* to double—makes it highly unlikely that he did so.

[2] Compare 4.1/4.3 where, because of the omission of 4.2, Gloucester exits with Henry and then immediately re-enters with the other nobles. (In F he speaks the first line of the scene, 'Where is the King?'—a ludicrous question, if 4.2 is omitted. Q omits the question and Bedford's reply.) In any case the so-called law of re-entry is most often disregarded in battle scenes. See, for instance, Act 5 of *Julius Caesar*.

[3] 'This scene provides three specific examples in which Q is deliberately altered to exclude the three lords. To attribute such precision in abridgement to the vagaries of an actor's memory is to seek an illogical explanation in place of a logical one' (Robert E. Burkhart, *Shakespeare's Bad Quartos: Deliberate Abridgements Designed for Performance by a Reduced Cast* (The Hague and Paris, 1975), 78). Burkhart's book is for the most part rendered useless by his decision to count characters per scene, rather than actually casting the plays; by his emphasis on comparing Quarto and Folio; by his systematic disregard for stage directions; and by the overstatement of his thesis, which offers abridgement and memorial corruption as alternative, rather than complementary, explanations. (That memorial corruption is at work in this quarto is clear from the species of nonsense pointed out by Daniel, which would preclude the use of the text as a prompt-book, and from the evidence accumulated by Alfred Hart in *Stolne and Surreptitious Copies: A Comparative Study of Shakespeare's Bad Quartos* (Melbourne, 1942), 190-202 and *passim*.) Burkhart has also been misled by his reliance on Greg's discussion of *Alcazar*.

and if the prisoners stayed on-stage for any time at all, it would also prevent any of the French from doubling Williams, who would then have to be taken by Gloucester.[1] This leaves Henry only two attendants. At least two are required, one to exit with Montjoy (l. 2647) and another to follow Fluellen. If we assume that four French prisoners were present, Exeter and Clarence could enter with Henry, as the '*Lords*' of the Q stage direction. Gloucester would play Williams, and could also enter with Henry. This would mean that, at Henry's entrance, there would be on stage six Englishmen (including Fluellen and Gower) and four French prisoners. This seems quite reasonable, and explains three further anomalies in the Quarto text. First, Q alters F's 'Our heralds' to 'our herald', a change which is entirely superfluous, unless the French prisoners enter in 4.7. Secondly, in 4.8 Q calls for Clarence, where the Folio has Gloucester. The character does not speak in the scene, and the change is pointless, unless we assume Gloucester was not available, because he was playing Williams. But unless the French prisoners appear in 4.7, Gloucester need not play Williams, and we would not expect him to do so, as it requires a rather hurried change in 4.1. Third, in 4.8 Q omits the entrance of the English herald, though actors are available. But if the French prisoners appear in 4.3, then Exeter or Clarence must serve as the herald whom Henry dispatches to bring him a list of casualties. Exeter and Clarence are both on stage in 4.8, and it would have been natural for the 'herald' of 4.7 to serve as the herald of 4.8—in fact, it may have been felt as a necessary corollary of the principle that the same character must be played throughout by the same actor. Exeter would thus have left the stage with Montjoy at 4.7.122 (2649), and in the next scene he would most naturally bring the list of casualties and prisoners with him, thereby rendering the herald of 4.8 superfluous, and necessitating the reallocation of his speech at 4.7.123 (2650) to Fluellen. In other words, if we assume that the reporter merely neglected to specify '*French prisoners*' in the relevant stage direction (and he has already, in 4.5, called for '*the four French lords*', so that '*King and the Lords*' might naturally in his mind include French as well as

---

[1] Henry's prayer in 4.1 is 18 lines long, and naturally spoken rather slowly and solemnly. If Williams were the first soldier off—as he often is, because of his irritation—he could leave at the beginning of Henry's 'clipper' lines, and the actor could speak Gloucester's first lines from off-stage. (Henry's response, 'My brother Gloucester's *voice*', at least suggests that he has just entered, at most.) I should emphasize, however, that the Williams/Gloucester doubling is not crucial to the adaptation hypothesis.

English noblemen), we can explain—what is otherwise inexplicable
—the reassignment of one speech from Exeter to Fluellen, the
wholesale removal of names from another speech, the omission of
one herald in 4.7 and another in 4.8, and the substitution of
Clarence for Gloucester in 4.7. It seems altogether unlikely that any
other factor could explain the conjunction of these five variables.

In the final scene the size of the cast again forces adaptation.
Isabel disappears, simply because there is no third boy to play her.
Henry, Exeter, Katherine, Alice, the French King, and Bourbon
speak; Pistol is excluded by his presence at the end of 5.1. This
leaves only two actors to play mute French and English lords, unless Fluellen and Gower reappear, *in propria persona*, as part of
Henry's entourage (or unless non-actors were pressed into service,
as mutes). This dearth of nobles probably explains the cutting of
Westmoreland's speech, and certainly explains the alteration of

> . . . Goe Vnckle *Exeter*,
> And Brother *Clarence*, and you Brother *Gloucester*,
> *Warwick*, and *Huntington*, goe with the King
>
> (3071–3)

to the Quarto's 'Go Lords' (G1, 18).

The hypothesis of a cast of eleven actors, two of whom were
boys, will thus explain: the omission of all but one of the Choruses;
the alterations in 2.2; the alterations in 2.4; the omission of 3.1; the
substitution of Bourbon for the Dauphin in 3.7 and 4.5 and the
consequent alteration of 3.5; the omission of 4.2; the omission of
Erpingham in 4.3; the substitution of Gloucester for Salisbury in
4.3; the transposition of 4.4 and 4.5 (probably); the five alterations
in 4.7 and 4.8; the omission of Isabel and of several English lords
from 5.2, and the consequent alteration of speeches in that scene. It
is also a prominent factor in explanations for the omission of the
Prologue and 1.1, the omission of Henry's final speech in 3.3, the
omission of the '*others*' in 3.7, and the extensive alteration of 4.1.
Moreover, the envisaged adaptation does not by Elizabethan
standards put an excessive burden on the cast, as can be seen by a
brief examination of the evidence of doubling in extant plots.[1]
Henry, Exeter, and Pistol each double only one other role—for
Exeter and Henry, doubling could be avoided altogether. Cambridge takes three other roles, Scroop two, and Grey four—but in

---

[1] See the excellent chapter, 'Doubling Patterns in the 1580's and 1590's', in
Bevington's *From* Mankind *to* Marlowe, 104-13.

each case, all but one of the roles is a single-scene appearance, and some are mute. Bardolph doubles three (assuming he appears in 5.2 as a mute French lord). The boy who plays the Hostess might seem over-burdened, taking five other roles, but of these, three speak a combined total of eight lines (even in the Folio), and his 'main' role appears in only two early scenes. In any case, this loading of the Hostess could be avoided, as it involves two arbitrary decisions: he need not double Court at all, and I have assigned him Le Fer (rather than Salisbury) simply to minimize the number of actors required to speak French. Only twice must an actor impersonate two different characters in a single scene—and this was, in any case, perfectly acceptable contemporary practice, so long as there was sufficient time to accomplish the change.

Though a fuller discussion will have to await the conclusions of the next chapter, we can now say with some confidence that the printer's copy for Q was not an annotated and abridged copy of a report of a full performance, as G. I. Duthie contended, but a straightforward (if corrupt) report of an abridged performance. As Greg said, in general this is intrinsically the likelier explanation anyway, because it is the simplest (*Abridgements*, p. 293). Duthie's hypothesis depended on the fact that he could find no positive evidence that any omission or alteration in Q was the result of the reporter having witnessed an abridged performance. We have now established that virtually every major change in the Quarto is the logical and clear consequence of an adaptation presupposing a reduced cast, and in these circumstances the hypothesis of an annotated report becomes superfluous. Of course, it would be possible to conjecture that all the required changes were made on the report itself, but the quantity of annotation has now become staggering, involving systematic recasting and including not simply the omission but the rewriting of passages, while other passages are left completely unintelligible, though the insertion of simple connective phrases would make sense of them. By Duthie's own admission the only positive evidence for this theory—the fact that the reporter was apparently familiar with passages which the Quarto omits—will admit of another and simpler explanation, that the reporter had earlier played in or witnessed a performance of the full version. As for the other details Duthie advances as proof, by his own admission they are complementary rather than conclusive, and each is easily explained by the nature of the abridgement. The omission of Ely's speeches in 1.2 is not proof that he should have been omitted from the opening stage direction, for an actor was easily available, and two bishops are more spectacular than one (particularly if 1.2 became the first scene in the play). It seems unlikely that Ely's speeches were omitted because the actor could not handle them, since the actor takes speaking parts elsewhere, and in fact of Ely's two speeches in the scene one disappears in a large cut that dispenses with several others as well, and the second is reassigned to a '*Lord*', a change which has the support not only of history but also, more importantly, of sense: Ely is present to support Canterbury's case, not contradict it. The omission of an exit for Fluellen and Gower at the end of 3.2 could, as Duthie himself admits, easily be due to the reporter; or it might indicate that the two scenes were run continuously, as is often done in the theatre. The omissions from the opening of 5.2 are, as we have already seen, cast-related; the poor reporting of the wooing can be explained by the progressive fatigue of the reporter's memory, and the difficulty for memorization of the material itself.

The 1600 Quarto is thus almost certainly a memorial reconstruction of an abridged text, designed for performance by eleven actors. But three variants in the Quarto require a different explanation, and that explanation is to be found in the official prompt-copy of the Chamberlain's Men, which must have intervened between Shakespeare's foul papers (the copy for F) and the prompt-copy for the abridgement (the ultimate source for Q). One of these anomalous details is the Quarto's conflation of Westmoreland and Warwick. The Quarto omits Westmoreland from 2.2, of necessity; it has also, apparently, deliberately omitted him from 1.2. In 4.3, his next appearance, his lines are given to Warwick. In the Folio Warwick speaks or is addressed only in 4.7, 4.8, and 5.2; he is called for in 1.2, but plays no part in the scene. The two parts are thus easily combined, and in fact in the play's post-Restoration theatrical history they almost always have been. Usually, Warwick is simply omitted from 1.2 and 5.2, and is replaced by Westmoreland in 4.7 and 4.8. The Quarto adopts the alternative and more difficult solution: Westmoreland disappears from 1.2, 2.2, and 5.2, and is replaced by Warwick in 4.3 (and possibly in the other scenes as well). In the first place it is odd that the Quarto has chosen the more complicated conflation, especially as the only difference is aesthetic. What's in a name? The scene in question, 4.3, contains Henry's list of names which shall be 'familiar . . . as household words': 'Harry the King, Bedford and Exeter, / Warwick and Talbot, Salisbury and

Gloucester' (2295-7). The one name omitted from this list is West-moreland, the man Henry began by addressing. As I have never seen this peculiar omission remarked upon, I trust the anomaly has gone unnoticed, and cannot be said unduly to distract an audience's atten-tion. But if the absence of Westmoreland's name from a speech originally addressed to Westmoreland goes unnoticed, the *presence* of Warwick's name, were the speech addressed to Warwick, would not pass unnoticed, but add a significant dramatic touch to the speech. Moreover, Westmoreland points backward to *Henry IV*; Warwick looks forward, as does the epilogue, to *Henry VI*. But of course Q omits the epilogue. These considerations in themselves suggest that the conflation of the two roles, and the decision to name the resultant character Warwick, antedates the abridgement. But there is in fact a further, and irrefutable, proof that it derives from the Chamberlain's Men's prompt-copy: substituting Warwick for Westmoreland in 4.3 seriously complicates the abridgement. If Westmoreland appears in 4.3, and Warwick in 4.7 and 4.8, the two roles can be played by different actors. But if Westmoreland dis-appears, and Warwick appears in 4.3, 4.7, and 4.8, he must be played in all three scenes by a single actor. Getting rid of a character does not always save an actor; here, it instead creates the need for one (just as adding a character, Bourbon, saved an actor). We have already seen that 4.3, and Warwick in particular, put a considerable strain on the adaptation, forcing one of the French to double Warwick, and to change during the excursions between 4.3 and 4.5. But if the Folio's Westmoreland were retained in 4.3, he could be played by Cam-bridge-Gower—an arrangement in every way preferable, from the casting point of view. To contend that the Westmoreland-Warwick conflation was a consequence of the abridgement, we must assume that the adapter deliberately abandoned the preferable alternative, for no discernible motive. But if the adapter inherited the confla-tion—if, that is, the roles had already been conflated in the original prompt-book—then the adapter's solution was the only one avail-able, and the purely aesthetic motives for naming the conflated character 'Warwick' are immediately intelligible, deriving as they must from the prompt-book of the play for London performances by Shakespeare's own company.[1]

---

[1] This does not necessarily mean Warwick was also substituted for Westmoreland in 1.2 and 2.2. Westmoreland's omission from 2.2 is a result of the reduced cast, and the evidence of 1.2 is ambiguous. Westmoreland's link with *Henry IV* would also be more relevant in these early scenes.

A similar problem occurs with 'Clarence', which is the Quarto's name for Bedford. This is made clear in 4.3, where Clarence takes Bedford's place, the text being altered to accommodate the change. In 1.2, in the Folio both Clarence and Bedford appear, though neither speaks; Clarence disappears thereafter. In the Quarto, only Clarence appears here; Bedford is not present in this or any other scene. In the Folio Bedford appears in 2.2; in the Quarto, his place is taken by Gloucester, not by Clarence. But this is a consequence of casting: Clarence is doubling with the Boy, and thus cannot appear in 2.2. All of Bedford's other Folio appearances occur in scenes omitted by the Quarto, but I think we would be justified in assuming that in the original prompt-book Clarence replaced Bedford throughout. Again, this has nothing to do with limitations of cast, and the reason for the change can only be aesthetic: Bedford is, as it happens, John of Lancaster, and someone has decided to exclude from Henry V's entourage this cold and distasteful creature from *Henry IV*, replacing him with the decidedly more likeable Clarence. I can imagine no one but an author who would bother about such trivia—an author, for instance, who had been initially misled by Lancaster's change of title, and who, having perhaps discovered his error in rereading Holinshed, proceeded to excise Bedford, replacing him with the first character who came to hand, the mute Clarence of 1.2.

Finally, the Dauphin. In the Folio, derived from Shakespeare's manuscript, the French King at the end of 3.5 orders the Dauphin to remain behind, when the army marches to Agincourt. Historically, the Dauphin was not present at the battle. However, by 3.7 Shakespeare had apparently changed his mind, for the Dauphin appears, without explanation, in the French camp. It appears then that the lines in 3.5 were a false start, very soon abandoned, and that being the case we would not expect them to survive in the prompt-book. That they did survive, however, is made almost certain by their appearance in the Quarto. Of course, in the Quarto they make excellent sense, for the Dauphin does not appear at Agincourt. But if the change to Bourbon was a mere expedient, necessitated by a small cast, how did the adapter get hold of those lines in 3.5? Either the lines had survived, anomalous as they were, in the original prompt-book,[1] or the adaptation was made by someone who

---

[1] The lines at the end of 3.5 have also, as a result of their presence in the Folio, survived in modern prompt-books; other than the Olivier film, I know of only one production (1937, Stratford) which omitted them. In the 1975 RSC production, at

consulted or remembered Shakespeare's foul papers—or the change to Bourbon was made in the original prompt-book.

I have tried to establish that Bourbon's appearance in the Agincourt scenes is inevitable, given a cast of eleven. If this were true the change could not reasonably be ascribed to the authoritative original prompt-book; it would be too difficult to dismiss the coincidence as a mere coincidence. But in fact, if the reasoning by which we arrived at that conclusion is examined carefully, an important logical flaw will become apparent, and this flaw, while it does not weaken the evidence for abridgement, does entirely reverse the conclusion about Bourbon, so that what before seemed proof that his appearance in the Agincourt scenes *must* have resulted from abridgement will emerge as proof instead that it did *not* result from abridgement, but antedated it.

The reader will recall that our original aim was to establish which actors played the three new characters (the Constable, the Dauphin, and the French King) introduced in 2.4. We had reduced the available actors to five: Henry, Gloucester, Cambridge, Scroop, and Grey. We assigned the Constable to Scroop, and then analysed the remaining four in greater detail, in order to establish the limitations on their availability created by previous and subsequent doubling responsibilities, and from that subsequent analysis we concluded that the actors available for the Dauphin in 2.4 and 3.5 were not available in 3.7 and 4.5: 'hence Bourbon'. But in fact *we could just as easily have assigned the Dauphin to Scroop*, and then the problem in 3.7 and 4.5 would not have been the Dauphin, but the Constable. In other words, with a cast of eleven either the Dauphin or the Constable had to disappear from those later scenes, to be replaced by Bourbon. But given this choice, it is inconceivable that any adapter would have sacrificed the Dauphin—the more important character, the one who insulted Henry in the first scene, the one Exeter defied in Act 2, the incarnation of French arrogance—in

scene's end the French King and his nobles left the stage in opposite directions, and after a pause the Dauphin followed the nobles, rather than his father (Sally Beauman, *The Royal Shakespeare Company's Centenary Production of* Henry V (Oxford, 1976), 158); perhaps this business is traditional, though I can find no other record of it. In productions which portray the French King as a feeble lunatic, the command would simply be further demonstration of the King's ineffectuality, particularly for an audience which *knew* beforehand that the Dauphin would appear at Agincourt. (This explains why the retention of the lines in modern productions is intelligible; it does not justify their retention in an edited text, unless we believe Shakespeare himself intended Charles VI as a madman—an interpretation with nothing but history to recommend it.)

order to preserve the identity of the Constable. We have no earthly reason to suppose that he consulted Holinshed, in order to 'get the facts'; we have even less reason to suppose that he would have heeded Holinshed at the expense of theatrical effectiveness. Moreover, the Dauphin is the unmistakable scapegoat of the play's patriotism; if he appears in 3.7 and 4.5, the structure of the play inevitably comes to depend in part on the contrast between him and Henry, a contrast which can only glorify the latter; and as the adaptation consistently labours to simplify the play's nationalism and heighten its glorification of Henry,[1] there is no reason to suppose that the adapter would have chosen the less simplistic of the two alternatives. His choice only makes sense if it was no choice at all: if, that is, the Dauphin had already been replaced by Bourbon in the unabridged version of the play from which he worked.

That Shakespeare had originally intended to absent the Dauphin from Agincourt is clear from the final lines of 3.5; we need only suppose that he reverted to this intention at some time between the composition of foul papers and the completion of the prompt-book. If we try for a moment to disregard our own familiarity with the Dauphin at Agincourt, it is easy enough to see why Shakespeare made the change. Structurally, Agincourt is improved by the Quarto arrangement, for Bourbon, unlike the Dauphin, does not fade from the play at its climax, but leads the critical second French assault, kills the boys, is captured, and thereby humiliated.[2] But—equally, if not more important—the Dauphin's previous history and his rank make him the inevitable focus for our attention in 3.7; the scene organizes itself around him, and consequently his arrogance becomes the keynote to our evaluation of all the French. To substitute Bourbon, a relatively new character, surrounded by his peers, radically reorganizes the energies of the scene: Bourbon is

[1] Besides its simplification of 4.1, the Quarto omits 1.1 (the mixed ecclesiastical motives for supporting Henry's claim to France), lines 115-35 of 1.2 (which culminate in the Archbishop's offer of church financing for the war), all references in 2.1 to Henry's personal responsibility for Falstaff's condition, Cambridge's hint of motives other than simple bribery for the conspiracy against Henry, the bloodthirsty MacMorris of 3.2, most of Henry's savage ultimatum in 3.3, and all of Burgundy's description of the devastation Henry has wreaked on France (5.2). The result is exactly the sort of simple patriotic play critics have often taken *Henry V* to be.

[2] It is at least worth remarking upon one incidental advantage of substituting Bourbon for the Dauphin. The list of French casualties at Agincourt includes 'Great Master of France, the brave Sir *Guichard Dauphin*' (4.8.97/2814); the risk of confusion, if the Dauphin appears at Agincourt, is obvious. The line has been often omitted, though usually in the context of a larger cut.

simply a single, if significant, figure in a larger and more complicated pattern, which includes the equally important scepticism and
professionalism of the Constable; the silence and peacemaking of
Rambures; the high spirits, common sense, and loyalty of Orleans;
the sense of humour of all three. To minimize the import of the man
who writes sonnets to his horse cannot but transform our entire
perspective on the French. Indeed, if the textual positions were
reversed, and Bourbon had appeared in the Folio, and the Dauphin
in the Quarto, critics would have been complacently remarking for
centuries upon the latter's vulgarity. The continued emphasis on the
Dauphin's role was, after all, something Shakespeare inherited from
that internationally acclaimed dramatic genius, the author of *The
Famous Victories of Henry the Fift.*

But the case for Bourbon is not only aesthetic. In the past the
issue has been clouded by the alternative theory that Q represents an
earlier draft of the play; but, as this theory has been long and justly
discredited, we must now account for the fact that someone, at a
very early stage in the play's history, deliberately substituted
Bourbon for the Dauphin, and our explanation for this fact must
also take account of four others: that Shakespeare himself (as the
Folio testifies) wavered over the Dauphin's presence; that whoever
was responsible for the abridgement knew three lines at the end of
3.5 that should have disappeared from the Chamberlain's Men
prompt-book, if the Dauphin appeared at Agincourt; that the
adapter, forced for casting reasons to split either the Dauphin or the
Constable into two characters, split the Dauphin, a decision wildly
improbable, if independently made; and that the aesthetic consequences of the change to Bourbon are of a kind diametrically
opposed to the effect of the adaptation throughout the remainder of
the text. All this evidence points to a single conclusion, the same
conclusion reached by aesthetic analysis: that the change to Bourbon antedates the abridgement, and was made by Shakespeare.[1]

---

[1] The substitution of Bourbon for the Dauphin creates difficulties only in 4.5,
where, in F, both characters appear. The simplest solution there would be to give
Bourbon the Dauphin's lines as well as his own; but this is not necessarily the correct
solution. As Bernard Beckerman has pointed out, in 'Shakespeare's Industrious
Scenes' (a paper given at the Eighteenth International Shakespeare Conference,
Stratford-upon-Avon, 1978), the dramatic structure of that scene in F depends upon
the energy of Bourbon—a new character, who does not speak in the first half of the
scene—overcoming the initial despair of the French, and turning their retreat into a
counter-attack. To give Bourbon his lines *and* the Dauphin's would destroy that
structure; more specifically, it would require Bourbon to propose, first, 'let's stab
ourselves' (4.5.7) and then 'once more back again' (11). Q removes that contradiction

We are now in a position to consider the vexing problem of Bourbon's appearance in 2.4. He is not called for in the Folio, but twice specifically named in the Quarto—once in the opening stage direction, and then in the French King's first speech, which is altered from the Folio to include Bourbon's name, and further altered to make the name an unmistakable direct address ('you Lords of *Orleans*, / Of *Bourbon*')—though he has nothing at all to say. In itself, this Quarto alteration makes perfect sense, as another of the preparations for Bourbon's major structural role at Agincourt. Here there are no loose speeches he can be given (as in 3.5), but he appears, the French King addresses him, and consequently it seems natural that he should reappear and speak in 3.5. However, with a cast of eleven, Bourbon in 2.4 cannot be played by the same actor who takes his part in 3.5, 3.7, and 4.5. We are thus confronted with three choices: either the Quarto text is wrong, or there were more than eleven actors available, or Bourbon was split between two actors.

The first of these alternatives is the least convincing. First of all, it involves us in the circular reasoning which we have condemned in Greg's discussion of *Alcazar*: the Quarto is right when it fits our hypothesis, but wrong when it does not. Moreover, in this instance the discrepancy is much more glaring than with the *others* direction of 3.6, because there can be no question of using stagehands or supernumeraries, or of an 'optical illusion'; we must instead explain away the call for a specific individual, in a stage direction and then in the text of the scene—a scene where one of the reporters (Gower)

by omitting line 7; but it also omits lines 4–10$\frac{1}{2}$, puts 19–21$\frac{1}{2}$ in their place, and assigns 19–21 to the Constable instead of Orleans. This produces an entirely different structural effect: not the Folio's contrast between the shamed confusion of their entrance and the despairing purpose of their exit, but a new contrast between the Constable's appeal to military reason ('We are enow yet living in the Field, / To smother vp the English in our throngs, / If any order might be thought vpon') and Bourbon's fatal despair ('The devil take order'), who in seeking relief from his personal humiliation advocates military suicide. Moreover, the Quarto in consequence of this rearrangement omits 'Be these the wretches that we plaid at dice for?' and 'Is this the King we sent too, for his ransome?', thereby removing the complacency of the original scene's irony, which relishes the simple contrast between their former arrogant hopes and their present humiliation. Of course, the Quarto's omission of these two lines, and its assignment of 19–21 to Orleans, could be the result of mere memorial corruption, for neither change is necessary; but given the Quarto's substitution of Bourbon for the Dauphin, it is much more difficult to believe that the omission of lines 7 and 10, or the transposition of 19–21, is fortuitous, and that defects of memory have thereby accidentally solved the very problems created by an earlier conscious revision.

was on-stage, and must have entered with the character in question. In the circumstances we must assume that Q is right, and resort to one of the two alternative explanations.

Appendix B contains a casting-chart for the Quarto text, based on the hypothesis of twelve actors; for that hypothesis, once invoked to explain this difficulty, obviously has consequences for the casting of the entire play. The advantages of a hypothesis of twelve actors are:

(1) it removes the (major) difficulty occasioned by Bourbon's appearance in 2.4;

(2) it removes the (minor) problem of the stage direction '*others*' in 3.6;

(3) it allows the actor who plays the Dauphin to double Warwick, thus eliminating the need for a rapid change in the (presumed) excursions between 4.3 and 4.5; as a result, we need not assume that the change from Westmoreland to Warwick in 4.3 antedated the abridgement, and the transposition of 4.4 and 4.5 can be explained on purely mechanical grounds;

(4) it relaxes doubling responsibilities throughout the play.

With the exception of (1), none of these is particularly persuasive in itself; (3) removes the need for an antecedent layer of revision at one, and perhaps two, points in the text, but this would only be significant if we could dispense with that layer of revision altogether, which we cannot, because the hypothesis of twelve actors makes the Dauphin–Bourbon change impossible to explain in any other way. With twelve actors, 3.7 and 4.5 could be played as they stand in the Folio; there is no mechanical reason at all for Bourbon's presence in 2.4 or 3.5 or 3.7, or for the revision of 4.5. Alternatively, if King Henry did double the Dauphin in 2.4 and 3.5 (which he need not), there would have been no need to omit any of the Choruses, which could all be played by Gloucester; if the Choruses had not yet been written, or were omitted on other grounds, there would be no earthly reason to make Henry double the Dauphin in 2.4 and 3.5. If he did not, there would be no need to omit 3.1. Moreover, the hypothesis of twelve actors leaves entirely unexplained the alterations in 2.2, 2.4, and 4.7, and the omission of 4.2; it forces us to suppose that the Quarto errs in omitting an *exeunt* for Fluellen and Gower at the end of 3.2; it forces the Hostess–Alice to double Fluellen, and creates a severe problem between 5.1 and 5.2, where Fluellen has only ten lines in which to exit and then re-enter *as a woman*. In short, the hypothesis of twelve actors creates as many casting problems as it solves, and also fails to account for a good many striking and otherwise inexplicable features of the Quarto text, which would all be explained by the assumption of eleven actors.

It seems to me then that the only reasonable solution to the casting problem created by Bourbon in 2.4 is to assume the role was there taken by another actor. As I have already pointed out (p. 94), such role-splitting does occasionally occur, and therefore its presence here should not put an intolerable strain on the credulity of seventeenth-century provincial audiences or sophisticated twentieth-century bibliographers. For the splitting makes excellent sense, given a cast of eleven and a text where Bourbon had already replaced the Dauphin at Agincourt. (If Bourbon had not already done so, in the text from which the adapter was working, there can have been no reason whatever for introducing him here, regardless of how many actors the adapter had at his disposal; if he only had eleven, there would have been the most compelling reasons *not* to add him to 2.4.) In those circumstances it would have been undesirable to omit him, or to change his name, because of Bourbon's overriding importance to the structure of Acts 3 and 4. Moreover, because he does not speak, he can be identified as a significant presence ('you Lord . . . Of *Bourbon*'), without calling excessive attention to his features or his voice; he will be to the audience simply a name, a costume, a particular cut of beard or colour of hair. The splitting of the role between two actors thus, at a very small price, preserves a detail of considerable importance to the plot and structure of the entire play.

It would of course be easier for the investigator and the reader if such complications did not arise at all; but historical phenomena seldom show much regard for the convenience of subsequent investigators. The investigator, however, should have some regard for the convenience of his readers. To summarize and recapitulate, then: Bourbon's appearance in 2.4 creates a dilemma; there are only three possible solutions to that dilemma; therefore, one of them *must* be right. The first is to regard the Quarto's identification as an error; this is possible, and would of course remove the problem completely, but it seems relatively unlikely, and in any case a weak support to fall back on. The second is to posit a twelfth actor; but there is no convincing evidence of his presence elsewhere, and the assumption creates new difficulties of its own, while leaving unexplained the most important features of the Quarto text. The third is to assume that in this scene the mute Bourbon was played by a different actor, in accordance with a practice documented elsewhere: this solves the casting problem in 2.4, makes excellent sense theatrically, and allows us to retain the hypothesis of eleven actors, which explains so many disparate and major variants. The third alternative therefore seems to me far and away the most likely solution. But *whichever* of the three alternatives we adopt, Bourbon's presence in 2.4 strongly supports the other evidence that the substitution of Bourbon for the Dauphin must have preceded the abridgement.

The alternatives offered editors by these six characters—Warwick, Westmoreland, Clarence, Bedford, Bourbon, and the Dauphin—form part of a larger problem, the treatment of French and English nobles throughout the play. The stage directions of the Folio text provide the most convincing evidence of its having been printed from foul papers.[1] They repeatedly call for the presence of characters who play no part in the action; they introduce new names for no apparent reason; they omit mention of characters in scenes where their presence would be not only logical but useful (Cambridge, Scroop, and Grey among the English nobles in 1.2). If editors do not clarify the play's confusion of French and English nobles, producers will, and the seeming chaos of Quarto and Folio in the distribution of those parts and the arrangement of those scenes has justified the most eccentric licences in the staging of the play. *Henry V*'s record of theatrical success and critical disfavour is not entirely unrelated to the fact that audiences have usually been given a more coherent version of the play than readers. Actors and producers have faced, and to the best of their ability solved, difficulties and contradictions in the text which editors have been content blithely to preserve, as though Shakespeare had personally overseen the publication of the play in the Folio. Though theatrical solutions have often been wildly wrong, they represent the honest attempts of laymen to cope with textual difficulties which the professionals should long ago have solved for them.

Who made the adaptation? According to Chambers, it is likely

---

[1] In fact the combination in the Folio text of accurate speech ascriptions and an accurate text with unreliable stage directions exactly parallels the condition of *Sir Thomas More*; as Scott McMillin has persuasively argued ('*The Book of Sir Thomas More*: A Theatrical View', *Modern Philology*, 68 (1970), 10–24), these characteristics argue for a manuscript from which the actors' parts were transcribed, in preparation for rehearsal, before the fair copy was made and submitted for licensing.

that the Chamberlain's Men did some touring in 1600,[1] and the size
of the cast supports the provincial hypothesis.[2] But the presence or
absence of external evidence is not crucial. The Quarto itself is proof

---

[1] Chambers, *WS* i. 64–5. There is evidence of a performance about this time in
Oxford, though of what and by whom we do not know (ii. 323).

[2] J. T. Murray, *English Dramatic Companies 1558–1642*, 2 vols. (London, 1910), i.
88: 'The usual number of actors in a travelling company of any importance seems to
have been ten or eleven.' (This is said in the context of doubts about whether a list of
only *eight* actors could have represented the whole touring company.) Unfortunately,
for corroboration of this generalization Murray refers the reader to his own 'English
Dramatic Companies in the Towns outside of London, 1550–1600', *Modern Philology*, 2 (1904), 539–60, where it transpires that he can provide only one piece of
evidence, a Leicester record of 1583 which lists ten actors as composing the touring
company of Worcester's Men (p. 556). Murray's reasoning is, however, more
persuasive than his evidence. 'Undoubtedly a company while travelling would present
only such plays as could be acted by an average number of players, and so do away
with the expense of taking with them actors for unimportant parts' (p. 557)—
especially as Murray elsewhere in the article provides convincing documentation for
the commonsense proposition that companies made less money in the provinces than
in London, and that these profits were further reduced by travelling expenses, and
their inability to play on some days, when between towns. Chambers, while admitting
that the evidence is scanty, observes 'The strength of seven companies which visited
Southampton in 1576–7 (Murray, ii. 396) ranged from 6 to 12. I incline to agree with
Murray and W. J. Lawrence (*TLS*, 21 Aug. 1919) that the average may be put at
about 10 for the latter part of the sixteenth century and that it grew in the
seventeenth' (*ES* i. 332, n. 1). Alwin Thaler, in 'The Travelling Companies in
Shakespeare's England', *Modern Philology*, 17 (1920), also concluded that provincial companies averaged from ten to twelve performers (p. 502). To this may be
added the circumstantial evidence of the cast list in the 1607 edition of *The Fair Maid
of the Exchange*, which is prefaced by the statement (false, as it happens), 'Eleauen
may easily acte this Comedie' (Lawrence, p. 74). That this claim is misleading makes
it all the more probable that the publisher had some motive for wanting to advertise
its suitability for such a small cast, and some reason for choosing the figure 11.
Nevertheless, Bradley (p. 13) disputes these assumptions about the size of touring
companies, pointing to a company of twenty-six or twenty-seven at Norwich on 10
March 1635 and to a letter of protection granted in 1624 to twenty-one hired men and
attendants of the King's Men (G. E. Bentley, *The Jacobean and Caroline Stage*, 7
vols. (Oxford, 1941–68), i. 15). These examples are, of course, from a later period. But
Bradley also observes that, in 1592, Strange's company petitioned the Privy Council
for leave to play in London, on the grounds of its great size, and he thinks it odd that
'this has . . . been taken as evidence that travelling companies were commonly small'
(p. 13). But unless travelling companies commonly *were* small, Strange's company
could not have hoped for exceptional treatment on the grounds of its size. In fact,
the wording of the petition strongly supports Murray's economic argument:
'Forasmuche . . . oure Companie is greate, and thearbie our chardge intollerable, in
travellinge the Countrie' (Chambers, *ES* iv. 311–12). In conclusion, we have every
reason to suppose that a travelling company would attempt to minimize its numbers,
and that, for 1599–1600, eleven actors is a reasonable number to postulate for such a
company. (It is worth remembering that this provincial tour need not have involved
the Chamberlain's Men; they could have sold the provincial rights to one of the
country companies.)

that within a year of *Henry V*'s première it was performed in an
abridged version by someone somewhere. I do not believe that the
abridgement itself was a piracy, for in the absence of evidence to the
contrary, there is no reason to suspect its being performed by
anyone but the company that owned it: either the Chamberlain's
Men, or a provincial company to whom they had sold the touring
rights.[1] It is difficult to imagine why such an abridgement would
have been performed anywhere but in the provinces, especially
as certain alterations presume a less sophisticated audience: the
simplification of 4.1, and Katherine's simultaneous translation of
Henry's French in 5.2, are prime examples. The abbreviation of the
play also supports this hypothesis. Of course, with a reconstructed
text it is exceedingly difficult to disentangle theatrical cuts from
memorial omissions, but if we count only the omissions of whole
phrases, speeches, and scenes, which leave no traces of contamination, and could be intelligibly removed from the text, the Quarto
shortens the Folio by over 1,200 lines.

For the editor of *Henry V*, the proof that major alterations in the
Quarto are merely the mechanical consequence of a limited cast will
be reassuring, for it will allow him to disregard those variants with a
good conscience. But paradoxically, having established that so
many Quarto variants are the consequence of abridgement or
memorial error, we must begin to take very seriously indeed the
variants which cannot be so explained: the conflation of Warwick
and Westmoreland, the rechristening of Bedford as Clarence, the

[1] Three kinds of 'piracy' should be distinguished: theft of the text for performance
by an unauthorized company, theft of the text by a reporter for the purposes of
publication, and illegal publication. Memorial corruption does not, in itself, require
any of the three: it presupposes only the production of a text by a person or persons
not at that time in possession of a scribal text of the play, and the subsequent sale of
this memorial reconstruction, for whatever reasons. Of course, these conditions are
most easily fulfilled if the absence of a scribal text results from the memorial text
having been produced by unauthorized persons, for the purpose of unauthorized
performance and/or publication. However, even in this hypothesis, 'unauthorized'
should probably be defined as 'undesired' (by the original owners) rather than
'illegal'. In general, one might say that a memorial reconstruction is innocent until
proven guilty, and that, if proven guilty, one should presuppose the smallest possible
number of crimes: in this case, 'theft' by the reporter(s), for the purposes of sale to a
publisher. On the matter of publication see—generally—Leo Kirschbaum's *Shakespeare and the Stationers* (Columbus, Ohio, 1955), K. B. Danks's 'The bibliographical
and psychological fallacies in Pollard's second proposition' (*Notes and Queries*, 204
(1959), 439-40), and—specifically—the discussions of the *Henry V* staying entry
by Richard Knowles in the New Variorum *As You Like It* (New York, 1977),
353-64, and Thomas Berger's 'The Printing of *Henry V*, Q1', *The Library*, VI, 1
(1979), 114-25.

substitution of Bourbon for the Dauphin. And if the stage directions of the Quarto are as accurate as this investigation suggests, then the agreement of Q and F, against the editorial tradition, argues strongly that the editorial tradition is wrong, or at the very least in need of re-examination.

Four rather more general conclusions suggest themselves. From the perspective of Shakespeare studies, the success of this method of investigation in explaining so many unexplained anomalies in the Quarto of *Henry V* suggests it might be of similar value in resolving similar textual tangles in other plays, namely those preserved in bad quartos.[1] It might also prove useful in explaining certain anomalies and contradictions, like Mortimer's disappearance from *1 Henry IV*, if it appeared that such considerations of cast influenced Shakespeare's own treatment of structure. From the perspective of bibliography, it should be troubling that this technique, which has been available since at least 1922, and which Greg specifically developed and employed to analyse abridgements, had never been applied to the Quarto of *Henry V*, which has long been regarded as just such an abridgement. From the perspective of theatrical history, the Quarto represents, if I am right, an acting version, textually corrupt, but nevertheless of immense importance in suggesting how Shakespeare's plays were affected by theatrical necessity and theatrical fashion even in his own lifetime. The preparation and publication of an edited text, specifically for the needs of theatre historians, which preserves the casting, staging, additions, and omissions of the Quarto, but which perhaps corrects its dialogue by reference to the Folio (only, of course, when the variant is unmistakably the result of memorial corruption), should be a high priority—higher, for instance, than the production of yet more facsimiles of nineteenth- and twentieth-century prompt-books. Finally, from the perspective of aesthetics, the Quarto, and the entire Elizabethan system of doubling, raise the intriguing possibility that the structure of Shakespeare's play was influenced and possibly improved by the imposition of a purely mechanical restraint on the freedom of his imagination—the same kind of mechanical restraint, in fact, which limited Aeschylus, Sophocles, and Euripides.

[1] Scott McMillin, in 'Casting for Pembroke's Men: The *Henry VI* Quartos and *The Taming of A Shrew*', *Shakespeare Quarterly*, 23 (1972), 141-60, explains a number of characteristics of these quartos in terms of casting. Unfortunately, he presents conclusions, rather than a complete analysis of the supporting evidence, and therefore I cannot endorse his theory until I have cast the plays myself.

CAST CHART FOR THE QUARTO TEXT: ELEVEN ACTORS

The following chart is intended as a rough summary of the conclusions described and defended in detail in the essay itself; like most summaries, its only value is convenience. Thus, no attempt has been made to indicate by spacing where in the course of a scene a character enters or exits, and for an explanation of why Actor 11 can appear as Clarence in 1.2 and Boy in the next scene, a reader must refer either to the foregoing pages or to his own knowledge of the play.

The actors have been identified by number and by a name from 2.2/2.3, where the presence of eleven is first established. Where their presence in a scene is inferential, it has been enclosed in parentheses. A number of allocations of specific actors to specific roles is arbitrary, for the role might have been taken by someone else: for instance, the Messenger in 3.7 could be played by almost anybody. There might be some value in attempting to distinguish these typographically, but as this would create difficulties in differentiating degrees of arbitrariness, and would probably distract more than clarify, I have felt it best to leave such distinctions to the essay itself.

Orleans raises a small problem which was not discussed in the essay, but which perhaps deserves a mention here. The French King at the start of 2.4 addresses three named 'Lords' ('Dukes' in F1; Q1's 'Lords' is probably a memorial error). In addition, the Constable, who is not addressed, speaks. It is generally assumed that the Constable is not one of the three addressed lords or dukes, as historically he was not. But 'Constable' was simply an extra title for a man who must also have had some other noble title (without which he would never have become Constable). Thus, in *Henry VIII* 2.1.102 'When I came hither I was Lord High Constable and Duke of Buckingham'. So there would have been no difficulty for an audience—or a plotter for that matter—in assuming that 'the Constable' was one of the three addressed lords. From a purely logical standpoint, he can only have been Berri (for both Orleans and Bourbon will appear in later scenes with the Constable). But at this point such an identification would be extremely artificial, for in this scene there is nothing to identify any of the three names with any of the three lords on-stage, only one of whom even speaks. Bourbon is not identified until 3.7, and Orleans is not identified at all in the dialogue of Q, though F's text of 3.7 does name him, in a line that the reporter might simply have forgotten to include. What all this means is that neither an audience nor the plotter himself nor the actors could be expected to realize that any problems would be created by the loose attribution of one of those names in 2.4 to the Constable, and that the problems which are created are invisible to all but the most microscopic—one might say pedantic—scrutiny.

	Actor's role in 2.2/2.3	1.2	2.1	2.2	2.3	2.4	3.2	3.3	3.4	3.5
1	HENRY	Hen		Hen		Dau		Hen		Dau
2	EXETER	Ex		Ex		Ex		(Ex)		
3	GLOUCESTER	(Gl)		Gl		Fr King		(Gl)		Fr King
4	SCROOP	Att		Scr		Cons				Cons
5	CAMBRIDGE	Ely		Cam		Bour	Gow	(Gow)		
6	GREY	Cant		Grey		(Berri)	Flu	(Flu)		
7	PISTOL	Amb	Pis		Pis		Pis	Gov		
8	BARDOLPH		Bard		Bard		Bard			
9	NYM		Nym		Nym		Nym			Bour
10	HOSTESS	Mute Amb	Host		Host				Alice	
11	BOY	Clar	Boy		Boy		Boy		Kate	

3.6	3.7	4.1	4.3	4.5	4.4	4.6	4.7	4.8	5.1	5.2
Hen		Hen	Hen			Hen	Hen	Hen		Hen
(Ex)			Ex			Ex	(Ex)	Ex		Ex
Gl		Wms/Gl	Gl			(Gl)	Wms	Wms		Fr King
	Cons			Cons			(Cons)			Fr Lord
Gow		Gow				(Gow)	Gow	Gow	Gow	
Flu		Flu	York			(Flu)	Flu	Flu	Flu	
Pis/Mont		Pis	Mont		Pis	Pis	Mont		Pis	
	Orl	Bates	Sal	Orl			(Orl)			Fr Lord
	Bour		Warw	Bour			(Bour)	Warw		Burg
	Geb	Court		Geb	Le Fer?		(Geb)			Alice
Clar	Mess		Clar		Boy		(Clar)	Clar		Kate

CAST CHART FOR THE QUARTO TEXT: TWELVE ACTORS

THIS chart is intended to describe in detail the possibility—discussed in summary on page 106, and there rejected—that the Quarto text was designed for performance by a cast of twelve. The methodology by which this chart was constructed, and the facts of the text, are the same as for the preceding chart.

#	Actor's role in 2.2/2.3	1.2	2.1	2.2	2.3	2.4	3.2	3.3	3.4	3.5
1	HENRY	Hen		Hen				Hen		
2	EXETER	Ex		Ex		Ex		(Ex)		
3	GLOUCESTER			Gl		Fr King		(Gl)		Fr Kin
4	SCROOP	Att		Scr		Con				Co
5	CAMBRIDGE	Ely		Cam		Berri	Gow			
6	GREY	Cant		Grey		Dau				Da
7	BOURBON	Att				Bour				Bo
8	PISTOL	Amb	Pis		Pis		Pis	Gov		
9	BARDOLPH		Bar		Bar		Bar			
10	NYM		Nym		Nym		Nym			
11	HOSTESS	Mute Amb	Host		Host		Flu		Alice	
12	BOY	Clar	Boy		Boy		Boy		Kath	

	3.7	4.1	4.3	4.5	4.4	4.6	4.7	4.8	5.1	5.2
		Hen	Hen			Hen	Hen	Hen		Hen
		Court	Ex			Ex	Ex	Ex		Ex
		Wms/Gl	Gl			(Gl)	Wms	Wms		Fr King
	Con			Con			(Con)			Fr Lord
w		Gow					Gow	Gow	Gow	
		Bates	Warw			(Warw)		Warw		(Warw)
	Bour			Bour			(Bour)			Burg
nt		Pis	Mont		Pis	Pis			Pis	
	Geb			Geb			(Geb)			Fr Lord
	Orl			Orl			(Orl)			Eng Lord
		Flu	Sal/York		Le Fer		Flu	Flu	Flu	Alice
r			Clar		Boy		(Clar)	Clar		Kath

W. W. GREG AND
THE BATTLE OF ALCAZAR

GREG himself, in a footnote, conceded the potential circularity of his procedure (p. 45, n. 1), but despite his consciousness of the danger he succumbs to it repeatedly. As a full reconsideration of the *Alcazar* problem would itself take an article, if not a book, and as I understand that David Bradley has in fact completed such a book, I will here limit myself to illustrating a few of the more important weaknesses in Greg's argument. For *Orlando Furioso* Greg possessed an alternative good text, in the form of Alleyn's manuscript part, and he was thus able to establish the (hypothetical) memorial corruption of the printed by comparison with the (presumptive) accuracy of the manuscript text. For *Alcazar* Greg had no alternative text; he had only the 1597 Quarto and a plot for the first four Acts. This plot itself contains a good many obscurities, and at the very best could only offer information about the accuracy of the stage directions in the printed text. There can be no certainty about the authority of the plot itself, since as its date makes clear, it belongs to a posthumous revival; furthermore, David Bradley has challenged Greg's crucial assumption that plots were used to regulate performances, arguing instead that they can have functioned usefully only in rehearsals (Bradley, 10–12). In any case, Greg is faced with two documents of uncertain authority, uncertainly related, and overlapping only in small part. That area of overlap is, moreover, one inevitably beset by ambiguity and instability. Memorial stage directions are in most respects indistinguishable from certain authorial or prompt-book types; authorial directions are themselves often indistinguishable from prompt-book types. Theatrical production—particularly the revival of so spectacular a play—is as likely as not to involve alterations in staging, including the addition or omission of scenes, dumbshows, and speeches. Casting too may make its demands. In the circumstances, the wisest course would have been to attempt to establish the character of Q on purely internal grounds, without reference to the plot at all, and then, on the basis of whatever conclusions had been reached, to attempt to reconstruct the text's relationship to the plot. This Greg did not do, and in retrospect it is easy to see why he did not: he had set out to lay empirical foundations for the theory of abridged texts, and to have wholly abandoned his one piece of empirical evidence (the plot) would have returned him to the realm of mere bibliographical speculation. But whatever historical excuses we make for Greg, the fact remains that, in using the plot to prove the (intelligible) Quarto corrupt, and then using the Quarto to correct and interpret the (corrupt) plot, he has committed a grievous error in logic. Thus, he assumes that any alexandrine, or four-foot line, or fragment of prose is a metrical corruption, and presumptive proof of omission; that any textual crux, however easily emended, is evidence of omission or incomplete adaptation; that, if a required word or line is missing from the text, we are justified in assuming that a number of other words or lines have also disappeared; that the absence of an exit results from the omission of an intervening passage of dialogue; and, most remarkably, that the presence in the Quarto of something not in the Plot is proof that something has been omitted *by the Quarto*—Q's 'Sound Trumpets' at 375 and 389 having been inserted to cover excisions (p. 108). In this last instance Greg avails himself of a suggestion of Dover Wilson's that the alternation of italic and roman stage directions in Q is evidence of different stages in the ancestry of the underlying manuscript, an hypothesis 'hardly sufficiently certain to form a satisfactory basis for further conjecture' as Greg himself said (p. 100); and yet the presence of roman stage directions is repeatedly taken as evidence of adaptation or omission, though in fact nothing in the context requires or even supports this presumption. Greg by such reasoning is driven to postulate, behind Q, *two* layers of revision, one incomplete, undertaken over the authorial manuscript itself; and even this tortuous hypothesis leaves much, by his own admission, unexplained. 'I find it difficult to imagine a motive for . . . removing any characters from the earlier scenes' (p. 122). In fact, the most striking instance of textual adaptation in the interests of casting comes not from the Quarto but from the Plot, for the one scene it omits (3.2) requires Massye, who played a Spanish ambassador in 3.1, to reappear immediately as Zareo (his regular part), and Humphrey Jeffs, who plays a captain in 3.3, to appear immediately before as Seth (his regular part). Similarly, the soliloquy which can be inferred from the Plot at the end of 2.3, besides being the kind of autonomous material most easily added in a revival, has the practical advantage of freeing the four actors for re-entry at the beginning of 2.4, where one of them (Hunt) is needed for a Moorish ambassador.

Greg's analysis is also repeatedly hampered by a rather poor sense of the theatre, a quality surely of paramount importance in any discussion of theatrical adaptation. He supposes that Zareo, specified by the Plot in the opening stage direction of 1.1, and of some importance later in the play, must have been omitted by the Quarto, which does not call for him in this scene, or give him anything to say; but if Q's vague collective direction for 'Moores and janizaries' were authorial—or memorial—it would be perfectly natural for a production (i.e. the Plot) to include Zareo in their number, and make him prominent either visually or by giving him something to say, precisely because he *will* be important later. Greg's alternative hypothesis presupposes that a theatrical adaptation produced a version less effective theatrically. Again, at 1.2.279, Greg thinks it improper that the messenger speaks before being addressed by Mahomet, and therefore he suspects an omission; as the Messenger enters crying 'Fly . . . flie, flie', such attention to etiquette could only be ridiculous in the theatre. This messenger, according to the Plot, is played by the same actor who marched off as Pisono earlier in the scene, but Greg insists that he must be regarded as a different character; in fact, it would be highly dramatic if Pisono *were* the messenger of his own defeat, and one suspects that Greg's dissatisfaction with this arrangement derives from an entirely unElizabethan concern for the time-scheme. Besides, even if the Plot version were judged 'cruder', it is cruder in an unmistakably theatrical way. In 2.4 Greg objects to the sudden conversion of Stukeley and his men, regarding its abruptness in Q as evidence of incompetent abridgement; in fact, a more dilated treatment, though perhaps appropriate for psychological tragedy, would be entirely inappropriate here. Stukeley makes it clear that they *want* to continue to Ireland; Sebastian then plays his trump (his physical power over them). What choice is left them? Sebastian appears at first to give them one, but only until it becomes clear that they will not choose as he wishes. In 3.4 the Plot has the Governor and captain enter at one door, and join with Portugal (who enters from the other) *before* the entry of the Moor, probably from the centre; from the Quarto one would gather that the first two entrances were combined. Again, the Plot offers the more spectacular arrangement, and one that would have required (at most) the addition of only a line of dialogue; one cannot imagine any theatrical adaptation that would deliberately and voluntarily invent the less effective version in Q. In 4.2 the Plot again preserves the more dramatic staging, which we are asked to believe was deliberately sacrificed for no more compelling reason than the desire to omit a few lines, which could have been painlessly spared elsewhere. Finally, Greg's failure of dramatic sympathy is nowhere more evident than in his treatment of the battles in the last Act, where he has no Plot at all for comparison; these he characterizes, in an entirely modern judgement, as 'mere scuffle and noise' (p. 118), presuming that they are mingled and abridged, though in fact they are not only perfectly coherent but even, by Elizabethan standards, rather fully dramatized.

The Battle of Alcazar may eventually prove of great value to the study of Elizabethan stage abridgements, but only if the status of the Quarto is first independently established, and Greg's work on its relationship to the Plot entirely redone. I suspect that in the end bibliography will stand Greg's interpretation on its head, and take the Plot as an adaptation of the Quarto; but until the matter is fully investigated afresh, we can have no confidence in any deductions based on either hypothesis.

CORRUPTION AND AUTHORITY IN THE BAD QUARTO

THE 1600 Quarto of *Henry V* is a memorial text. This was established by P. A. Daniel in 1877, and confirmed, with decisive thoroughness, by Alfred Hart in 1942 and G. I. Duthie in 1964.[1] But 'memorial' is not a synonym for 'worthless', as twentieth-century editors often seem to assume. Our texts of Homer are memorial, and every theatrical performance is a memorial reconstruction. Even the most conservative modern editors of *Henry V* have adopted a dozen or more readings from Q—though most have been grudgingly dismissed as corrections so obvious that they would have been made even if Q had never existed.[2] But, if Q proves itself right in cases where F is unmistakably wrong, it is equally capable of being right where F, though wrong, is possible; as Housman said, 'Chance and the common course of nature will not bring it to pass that the readings of a MS are right whenever they are possible and impossible whenever they are wrong.'[3]

The recognition of bad quartos as a distinct class of texts, sharing a range of characteristics and bearing witness to a common origin, launched a revolution in Shakespearian textual scholarship, but, like most great simplifications, this revolution at first overlooked and subsequently obscured certain relevant complexities. The reliability of a memorial text depends, obviously enough, upon the reliability of the memory or memories involved, and these will vary, not only from play to play—witness the varying quality of extant

[1] *Henry V: Parallel Texts of the First Quarto (1600) and First Folio (1623) Editions*, ed. B. R. Nicholson, with an introduction by P. A. Daniel (London, 1877); Alfred Hart, *Stolne and Surreptitious Copies: A Comparative Study of Shakespeare's Bad Quartos* (Melbourne, 1942); G. I. Duthie, 'The Quarto of Shakespeare's *Henry V*', in *Papers Mainly Shakespearian*, ed. Duthie (Edinburgh, 1946), 106-30.

[2] W. W. Greg, 'Principles of Emendation in Shakespeare', in *Aspects of Shakespeare*, by L. Abercrombie and others (Oxford, 1933), 168-9. Some of these corrections were in fact made by editors with no knowledge of Q: the insertion of *him* in line 716 (F2), *Masham* for *Marsham* (777—Rowe), the insertion of a word in line 805 (F2 *three*, Q1 *haue*), *lenity* for *Leuitie* (1560—Rowe), *countryman* for *countrymen* (2640—F2), *God* for *Good* (2645—F3), and *swear* for *swore* (2983—F3).

[3] Introduction to Manilius (1903), p. xxxii. Housman was discussing the manuscript transmission of classical texts, but his argument is relevant to all forms of textual transmission, and indeed to all forms of error.

bad quartos—but also *within* the play itself—as even the briefest
perusal of these texts demonstrates. In fact, the variations between
and within bad quartos have been the foundation of every attempt
to identify the reporters, their methods, and the circumstances of the
text's transmission. Nevertheless, the editorial corollaries of this
unevenness of quality have apparently escaped notice. What follows
is an attempt to notice them.

It must first be recognized that, although agreement of Quarto
and Folio testifies to the Quarto's accuracy, the presence of readings in the Quarto different from those in the Folio does not, in
itself, prove that the Quarto is corrupt, but only that it is different. As the preceding essay makes clear, many Quarto variants
are the result of a memory or memories faithfully recording the
text of a deliberately adapted version of the play. We may regard
that adaptation as a corruption or debasement of the author's
intentions—though our judgement in that case will be an entirely
aesthetic one—but, insofar as the adaptation has been faithfully
reported in Q, Q represents an accurate text of a different version
of the play. We must thus always allow for the possibility that
Q contains a record of conscious and deliberate alterations made by
the author himself, or by others, of the text preserved in the foul
papers used as copy for F.

Other variations between Q and F could be the consequence of
printing errors, rather than memorial corruption. The following
readings in Q seem safely attributable to this cause:

To his vnfurnish[t] nest	(A3^v, 14)
When we do rowse vs in [our] throne of *France*	(A4^v, 31)
parte [F: *parlas*; edd.: *parles*]	(C3, 29)
englatara [mislined]	(C3, 34)
che chevalires [F: *Seigneurs*]	(C3^v, 23)
Aloues [= Alones; F: *alons*]	(C3^v, 28)
if I had had a sow [F: if I had a Sow]	(D2^v, 30)
Pist. [not in F]	(D3^v, 12)
Godes sollud	(D4, 4)
Ony e [= Ouye]	(E3^v, 15)
Boy. [misplaced]	(E3^v, 20)
But I [had] not so much of man in me	(E4, 27)
I know the the gloue is a gloue	(F2^v, 12)
And thou thou hast giuen me	(F3, 1)
Nououes [= Nonoues; F: *Non nobis*]	(F3^v, 29)
Hate. [= Harry] Now *Kate*	(G1, 26)
Douck [= Donck]	(G1^v, 29)

These errors are obvious, and would have been corrected by any
editor of Q, even if F had never existed. But having conceded that
these errors originated in the printing house, we cannot dismiss the
possibility that other corruptions in Q may be the result of similar
compositorial, rather than memorial, error. A considerable number
of inferior readings in Q *could* be the consequence of compositorial
dittography, haplography, transposition, sophistication, or simple
substitution; of foul case errors, turned, transposed, or omitted
letters. The sheer number of such errors, and the known presence of
another agent of corruption, severely reduce the probability that *all*
of them are compositorial, but in any individual instance it will be
impossible to apportion responsibility.

Misreading, another obvious potential source of error, could have
occurred in the printing house, or during any of the scribal stages
which intervened between Shakespeare's foul papers and the written
parts of the actors in the abridgement. The following Quarto
readings clearly are, or *could* be, misreadings.

192	Elue F	*Elme* Q
241	imbarre F	imbace Q
607	combyne F	combind Q
843	hop'd F	hope Q
1032	masters F	musters Q
1341	*coudee* F	code, tude, cudie Q
1384	Sprayes F	spranes Q
1476	and F	one Q
1484	foot F	fate Q [='fote']
1540	looke F	like Q [='loke']
1546	perdition F	partition Q
1913	fewer F	lewer Q1 lower Q3
2009	guilt F	gift Q[1]
2011	Periurie F	Forgery Q
2153	Chauntries F	chanceries Q
2474	Whilst F	Why least Q [='Whylest']
2475	contaminated F	contamuracke Q
2813	*Rambures* F	*Ranbieres* Q
2978	limbes F	lines Q [='lims'][2]

The most important characteristic of misreadings, and compositorial error in general, is that F is as susceptible to such corruption

---

[1] Compare *Love's Labour's Lost* 2602 (M5ᵛ), where F's *gilt* is accepted as a
correction of Q1's *gift*.

[2] Unless Q1's reading represents 'loins', to which it was emended by Q3; *lines*
would be a legitimate contemporary spelling.

as Q. Therefore, for any variant readings which could be the result of printing error in F, the reading of Q should be treated no more, and no less, suspiciously than that of F. Another list of misreadings will perhaps illustrate this principle.

219	find F	fine Q
310	their F	your Q
359	And F	End Q, edd.
360	defeat F	defect Q
527	name F	mare Q, edd.
1340	Arme F	arma Q
1547	reasonnable F	reasonably Q
1560	Leuitie F	lenitie Q, edd.
1924	heare F	heard Q
2472	hence F	home Q
2640	Countrymen F	countryman Q, edd.
2983	swore F	sweare Q, edd.

In principle, the Quarto readings in the list which have been adopted by all editors are indistinguishable from those which have not, and any one of them might be preferred; indeed, Alice Walker strongly defended the first, and Greg the second.[1] In such cases, Q must be treated as a collateral substantive text, and its readings recorded, even if an editor finally rejects them. Indeed, even where it is clear that Q, and not F, contains the misreading (e.g. combine–combind), Q's testimony is important, as an independent indirect witness to the true text.

Misreadings are the easiest category of compositorial error for an editor to handle because the category can be sharply defined and limited, and clearly distinguished from memorial corruption.[2] But interpolation, omission, transposition, substitution, dittography, and aural errors could be the consequences of memorial or of compositorial error, and could affect any word of the text. If Q contains a word not present in F, its presence in Q may be the result of memorial interpolation, or its absence from F due to compositorial omission; an editor's decision will be based on his judgement of relative probabilities. But to date this weighing of probabilities

[1] Alice Walker, *RES* N.S. 6 (1956), 110; Greg, *Principles*, 174.

[2] It is often impossible to determine whether a variant results from misreading or foul case error. Nevertheless, the number of variants which *could* be misreadings can be strictly limited; so can the number which *could* be foul case errors, or due to compositorial omission, transposition, or interpolation of letters. That these lists will to some degree overlap is less important than the fact that each is strictly limited and involves a type of error which may have nothing to do with memorial transmission.

has taken the crudest possible form: an actor trying to remember a performance is likely to make far more errors than a compositor trying to remember the manuscript he has just read, therefore *whenever* Q and F differ in a manner which *could* be the consequence of memorial error in Q, unless F is impossible Q is wrong, and F right. A more sophisticated and a more satisfactory formula would be based upon (a) a thorough and detailed examination of the probability of defined types of error within distinct areas of Q, combined with (b) a thorough and detailed examination of the probability of defined types of error within the stints of different compositors in F, presided over by (c) an aesthetic and critical evaluation of the merits of each case. The third element can be provided only by the individual editor; the second, which of course would have repercussions beyond *Henry V*, has not yet been provided, though Alice Walker and Paul Werstine have made valuable contributions;[1] the first, which is the object of this investigation, must be based upon identification and evaluation of the reporting agent or agents behind the Q text.

The possibility that the agent or agents responsible for the transmission of Q had occasional recourse to a manuscript must also be considered. Duthie (pp. 117–19) has refuted the hypothesis that Gower's or Exeter's part was available. The two passages where manuscript authority seems most likely are the Governor of Harfleur's lines (1303–10) and the difficult piece of Latin and French in Exeter's final speech (3326–32). The latter, involving exactly the kind of material that might have been transcribed on a separate slip of paper for use on-stage, is particularly likely, especially if Exeter was one of the reporters. The manuscript authority for the Governor's speech would instead have to be the actor's part, and the case for its use is based on the accuracy of Q's substantives, and the similarity of its accidentals to F's. The Quarto's substantive accuracy will admit of a memorial explanation, as I will attempt to demonstrate hereafter; the Quarto's inaccuracy, involving two clear errors within seven lines ('Returnes vs word, his' for 'Returnes vs, that his'; 'defensiue now' for 'defensible'), makes manuscript

---

[1] Alice Walker, 'The Folio Text of *1 Henry IV*', *SB* 6 (1954), 45–60; Paul Werstine, 'Compositor B of the Shakespeare First Folio', *AEB*, 2 (1978), 241–64. Also relevant is E. A. J. Honigmann's 'On the Indifferent and One-Way Variants in Shakespeare', *The Library*, V, 22 (1967), 189–204. I have myself completed a concordance and analysis of agreed errors in all Compositor A's stints, and begun a similar study of B's work on the plays set from manuscript or annotated quarto copy.

authority unlikely. The punctuation evidence would admit of alternative explanations, Q contamination of F or dependence of Q and F upon the punctuation of the same manuscript. The theory of Q copy for F has already been refuted; it would be disingenuous to suppose that Q copy was used for these seven lines, but nowhere else. The second hypothesis involves similar improbabilities. As F was printed from foul papers, and Q can only have had reference to an actor's written part, the manuscript authority for F and that conjectured for Q must in any case have been separated by several stages of transcription. Moreover, if *Sir Thomas More* is representative, Shakespeare's foul papers probably contained the barest minimum of punctuation, so that F's pointing most likely represents the practice of Compositor A, not the accidentals of Shakespeare's manuscript. In short, we can only conclude that the agreement of Q and F in accidentals in these seven lines is the product of nothing more exciting than accident. Both Q and F contain three colons, identically placed; Q agrees with five of F's seven commas; excluding five emphasis capitals in F but not Q, all but two spellings are the same (Mercy/mercie, rayse/raise). The fact that this agreement can only be coincidental, and that the coincidence cannot even be attributed to origin in a common ancestral manuscript, should serve as a warning to bibliographers about the necessary value of evidence based on accidentals.

The reporter or reporters behind a memorial text can only be identified by an analysis of the distribution of error in the text. If the errors fall into significant patterns, associated with the roles of certain actors, then it seems reasonable to assume that those actors were engaged in the reconstruction.[1] In *Henry V* three possible identifications have been suggested: Exeter, Gower, and the Governor of Harfleur. But the third could have been doubled by either of the other two; or, alternatively, if Fluellen and Gower remained onstage during 3.3 (Q provides no exit for them, and in the theatre 3.2 and 3.3 are often thus combined), and if (as seems certain if Exeter did not himself double the Governor), Exeter were among Henry's

---

[1] Leo Kirschbaum, in 'An Hypothesis Concerning the Origin of the Bad Quartos' (*PMLA* 60 (1945), 697–715), argued that, because memorial errors occur *throughout* the texts, they cannot have been reported by actors. This hypothesis ignores palpable differences in the kind and frequency of error within the texts, and it takes the occasional agreement in accidentals of good and bad texts—like that in 3.3—as evidence of memorizing from a manuscript, without in any way explaining why it should be so occasional. The hypothesis has not been accepted by subsequent investigators.

nobles, the presence on-stage of both reporters, with nothing to do but listen, could in itself easily explain the accuracy of their report of the Governor's speech. For it is not only the Governor's speech which is well reported. In this scene the Quarto is guilty of two omissions. The first, of thirty lines (1270-1300) from the middle of Henry's long ultimatum, is a natural cut firmly endorsed by post-Restoration performances, and certainly inevitable in any abridgement of the play. The second omission (1311-18) is equally possible as a deliberate and coherent theatrical cut, especially as its content (sickness, retreat, fortification in expectation of a French counterattack) is of just the sort which the adapter elsewhere altered or omitted in the interests of simplifying the play into patriotism. If we disregard these two omissions the remainder of the scene in Q contains only four errors ('parley weele' for 'Parle we will', 'we' for 'I', 'be' for 'lye', and 'are' for 'shall be') in twelve lines, while the Governor's speech itself has at least two ('word' for 'that' and 'defensiue now' for 'defensible') and perhaps five ('succour' for 'Succours', 'not yet' for 'yet not', and 'dread' for 'great' may be right[1]) within seven lines. Investigators may have assumed that the accuracy of the remainder of the scene might be due to the Governor's presence, but in fact in Q, as in F, he does not enter until he speaks; modern editors reposition his entrance, but (for reasons I will explain hereafter) I believe they are wrong to do so. There is, then, no reason to assume that the Governor was involved in the transmission of the text, either as a third reporter, or as a role doubled by one of the other two.

Before proceeding any further, I had best remark on a potential circularity in my reasoning. I have said that a difference in reading between Q and F does not in itself prove that Q is wrong, and yet the identification of reporters is based upon precisely the opposite assumption, that where Q differs Q is wrong. This circularity has in fact invalidated a good many studies of bad quartos— as the preceding paragraph may indicate—and it can only be overcome by perpetual vigilance, a steady attention to the possibility that the reporter was accurately relating what he actually saw or heard. The most dramatic differences between what he witnessed and the text we know are no doubt due to his familiarity with an

---

[1] Alice Walker defended 'succour' and 'dread' in 'Some Editorial Principles (with special reference to *Henry V*)', *SB* 8 (1956), 100. The transposition could easily represent compositorial error, in F or Q, though the F order seems aesthetically preferable.

abridged and adapted version; on the nature of that version the preceding chapter attempts to shed some light. More generally, though, we must always be conscious of possible theatrical motives behind Q variants (particularly omissions). But there are other differences between Q and F which, though not attributable to deliberate theatrical alteration, may nonetheless not be attributable to the reporter either. Two categories of potential variant involve cases where Q would be right; that is, where Q preserves the author's final intentions, either by reporting accurately a reading corrupted in F, or by preserving an authorial revision made in the fair copy. These are precisely the variants we have set out to find, and it is impossible to identify them with any certainty before we have begun—particularly as their identification depends in part on the conclusions of a study of Folio compositors A and B, which does not as yet exist. Nevertheless, we have every reason to believe that the number of such variants will be small, in relation to the total number of variants between Q and F, and we can pay some attention (as I have tried to do in the discussion of 3.3) to cases where a purely critical judgement might prefer Q.

There is another difficulty in using the presence of error in Q as a means of identifying the memorial agent. The text of the version the reporter(s) knew no doubt contained an indeterminate amount of scribal error. Shakespeare's foul papers, which supplied the copy for F, must first have been transcribed for a fair copy, which would have served as a prompt-book; that prompt-book must then have been transcribed to form the prompt-book for the adaptation; that prompt-book must then have been transcribed to supply the actors' parts. Some errors must have occurred in each of these stages of transmission, though, without a knowledge of the scribes involved, we can form no usable estimate of their numbers or location. The parts must then have been memorized. Actors today, and presumably then, vary widely in the accuracy with which they memorize their roles. Thus, if an actor who was sloppy about verbal detail were himself one of the reporters, he might record his own role exactly as he performed it: sloppily. But the sloppiness of the performance should not be confused with the accuracy of the report, for once an actor has memorized a role, he usually sticks to its wording, even if that wording as originally learned contains in-accuracies. If this applies to the reporter's own role, it applies also to the roles of his fellow actors. It is important to recognize that any memorial errors in the performance of X will look like memorial errors in the reconstruction by Y, though Y may in fact have recorded exactly what X spoke. Then too we must allow for transcriptional errors in the reporter's own manuscript. This can take the form either of inattention, which is likely to be greatest in those parts of the play he feels he knows best (i.e. his own part),[1] or—if there are two reporters working together—of errors in dictation. Finally, the compositor or compositors who set the Q text presumably made some errors of their own, errors which would often be indistinguishable from memorial ones—for many compositorial errors are memorial ones, as the manuscript text must pass through the compositor's memory into print. To isolate the errors of any one agent in such a chain of transmission may seem hopeless. But in fact the errors of all the other stages of transmission differ from those of the reporter or reporters in that they should be randomly distributed throughout the text. We have therefore every right to expect that an examination of relative frequencies of error will enable us to identify the reporter or reporters. But a recognition of the probability of error in the intervening steps of transmission alerts us to the need to study *relative*, rather than gross, frequencies of error. That is, we should not be surprised to find errors in a reporter's own part, including compound errors, which occur when an error committed in one stage of transmission is conjecturally (and mistakenly) 'corrected' in a later stage.[2]

[1] This psychological assumption was confirmed by an experiment I undertook with the help of Richard Derrington, who played the Boy in the 1977 Stratford revival of the 1975 RSC production of *Henry V*. Derrington, who had not looked at the text since he memorized the role 18 months before (when it began its international tour) offered to attempt part of a memorial reconstruction immediately after a performance. In an hour and a half he reconstructed the Prologue, 1.1 (which had been heavily cut), 1.2 through the Salic Law speech and (at my suggestion) 2.3. In transcribing his own small part in 2.3 Derrington committed three errors (two substitutions and an interpolation); he never committed any of these errors on the eight occasions I witnessed his performance. Interestingly also, his transcription of one of his cues was no more than a poor paraphrase. There are, admittedly, important differences between Derrington's circumstances and those of an Elizabethan reporter. However, these differences should not affect the foregoing examples, nor are they so great as those afflicting Betty Shapin's experiment ('An Experiment in Memorial Reconstruction', *MLR* 39 (1944), 9–17), which involved an amateur actress, a text in prose rather than (easier to memorize) verse, and a play deliberately written in an archaic stage-dialect (rather than English as contemporary to the modern reporter as Shakespeare's was to the reporter(s) of Q).

[2] For a discussion of this important category of error, see Eugene Vinaver, 'Principles of Textual Emendation', in *Studies in French Language and Medieval Literature presented to Mildred K. Pope* (Manchester, 1939), 351–69.

Having conjured up these intervening stages of transmission in order to assist in the identification of reporters, we may in the process have made such an identification seem valueless. 'If the transmission of Q involves so many sources of potential error, what editorial value can its text have, even in those portions best reported?' This rhetorical question is based on a misapprehension. For Q, which is six (and for some of the text seven) stages removed from Shakespeare's foul papers, nevertheless in a number of cases undoubtedly preserves the correct reading, when F, only one stage removed from foul papers, preserves an error. Obviously, in judging the probability of error in F and Q, an editor must take account of the length of Q's stemma of transmission, but this will be decisive only with absolutely indifferent variants; elsewhere, an editor should guard against giving it excessive weight. After all, though six stages of transmission may be unusually high for Shakespeare, it would seem phenomenally low to editors of classical plays. Moreover, one of Q's stages of transmission—from foul papers to fair copy—might be authorial.[1] Finally, simply to compare six to one, and thereby conclude that F is six times likelier to be right than Q, is to commit the fallacy of constant variation,[2] and to ignore the fact that, in textual transmission, two wrongs do often make a right.

We may now return to the identification of reporters. The case we have already discussed—the accuracy of Q's text of 3.3—illustrates the importance of two factors in the analysis of the accuracy of a memorial reconstruction: the first, the influence of a second memory, which has witnessed the same scene, and can correct and stimulate the first; the second, an account not only of the number of errors, but of their type. Some errors are obviously more serious than others, and different types of error are useful to the investigator in different ways. This can be illustrated by a comparison of the first two scenes in the Quarto, 1.2 and 2.1. In the Folio, 1.2 runs to 269 lines, 2.1 to 120.[3]

[1] Indeed, I think that an examination of Q provides a sufficient number of superior readings to convince us that the transcription to fair copy *was* authorial—or, at the very least, that the prompt-book made from that fair copy contained second thoughts, or suggestions made by the actors and accepted by Shakespeare.

[2] See J. K. Walton, *The Quarto Copy for the First Folio of Shakespeare* (Dublin, 1971), 78, 135.

[3] These figures are based on the lineation of Walter's new Arden text (London, 1954; rev. edn., 1960). I have in each case subtracted from the totals any Quarto omissions which seem probably or possibly deliberate (41 lines 1.2, 7 lines 2.1). Some consideration must be given to the fact that the line count for 2.1 is based on prose.

	1.2	2.1
substitutions	130	58
transpositions	15	14
omitted words	4	10
omitted phrases	29+	34
misattributions	2?	1?
interpolations	6	23
paraphrase	3	1

This evidence must be interpreted with some care. Because 1.2 is in verse, it is less prone to minor verbal interpolations and omissions, which would disturb the metre; when omissions do occur, they may lead to compensatory substitution, in an attempt to repair the metre, or in drastic cases to paraphrase due to a breakdown in sense. Nevertheless, the relative frequencies of error per line do show a marked increase in omissions in 2.1, and a particularly marked increase in interpolations. But the most telling difference between the two scenes is in the character of the transpositions, a difference the statistics do little to indicate. The transpositions in 1.2 are of a minor kind, the reversal of a doublet ('hardiness and policy'), the misplacement of a vocative ('Therefore to France, my Liege') or an adverb ('As 'tis ever common'). Only once is the transposition serious: 'So may a thousand actions, once a-foot' (358), the conclusion of the Archbishop's argument, is transposed to form the conclusion of the bee-simile (352), and used to introduce the catalogue of similes beginning 'As many arrows . . .'. It then occurs again in its proper place; its second occurrence is verbally much more accurate than its first. As the phrase thus occurs twice, it might indeed be classified as an anticipation, rather than a transposition. But the transpositions in 2.1, besides being more numerous, are—with only four exceptions—far more serious, involving the transposition of whole sentences, of whole speeches, and of parts of speeches into other speeches. These transpositions in themselves establish that the reporter(s) had no role in 2.1, and this conclusion is confirmed by 2.3, in which all the same characters appear. In that scene, in sixty (Folio) lines there are two clear misattributions, two major transpositions, twenty-two omissions of phrases or sentences, including one that produces nonsense, three instances of paraphrase, and sixteen interpolations.

For the purposes of reporter-identification, the most valuable errors are major transposition, paraphrase, and misattribution; nonsense-producing omissions are also important, though, for reasons to be discussed hereafter, they must be treated with some care. The frequency of these errors, and their combination, make it clear that the reporter(s) had no part in the Eastcheap scenes (2.1, 2.3, beginning of 3.2, 4.4) or in the French scenes (3.4, 3.5, 3.7, 4.4, 4.5, middle of 5.2). Quarto variants in these scenes must, consequently, be treated with considerable suspicion—though even from these scenes editors have universally adopted three Quarto readings ('mare' for 'name' 527, 'enough' for 'enough to' 579, and 'by a slaue' for 'a base slaue' 2474), and another two are normally though not unanimously accepted (the attribution of 'How now, mine host Pistol' at 531 to Nym, and the insertion of Nym's 'I shall have my eight shillings I won of you at betting' after line 604). All five of these readings occur in pages set by Compositor B. (For 2.1, the end of 4.4, and 4.5, the least reliable parts of Q coincide with the least reliable parts of F, those set by B.)

By examining the entire text in this way, one can by a process of deduction identify with reasonable certainty the reporters behind Q. That both Gower and Exeter were involved in the reconstruction seems clear; that no one else was involved seems equally clear. Gower's role in Q—discounting any large omissions, involving parts other than his own, which are presumably deliberate—contains 39 lines. These 39 lines contain 2 transpositions, 9 words interpolated, 5 words omitted, 5 phrases omitted, 1 speech possibly omitted, 16 verbal substitutions, and 1 paraphrase. All but two of these errors are of the most trivial kind and, as Gower's part is prose throughout, minor verbal interpolations and omissions are predictable. The two more serious errors are the omission of a speech ('Here comes his Majesty', 2577)—though it is theatrically redundant, and may naturally have disappeared during performance—and the single instance of paraphrase, where Folio's 'Why, this is an arrant counterfeit Rascall' (1508) is transformed into Quarto's 'Why is this the Ancient you told me of?'. But this paraphrase is dramatically much more apt than the Folio version, for Gower has not spoken since Pistol's arrival, and the Quarto version of the line calls our attention to his silence, explains it, reminds us of Fluellen's praise of Pistol before his entrance, and avoids the slight awkwardness of the Folio's 'this is . . . a rascal', spoken of someone not on-stage.

If our reconstruction of the casting of the Quarto abridgement is correct, the actor who played Gower must have doubled at least one other speaking role, that of a traitor in 2.2. This scene, for which

Exeter was also present, contains a number of neat and apparently deliberate omissions (630-5, 646-7, 649-53, 655-7 ('there's . . . gouernment'), 660, 698, 734-71, 784-94, 799-802, 816-20); at least, these omissions are all theatrically intelligible, some arguably improving the scene, and their very neatness makes inadvertence seem highly unlikely. Moreover, the supposition that they represent deliberate cuts is strengthened by the excellence of the reporting in the lines which are preserved. Any attempt to identify the reporter or reporters for this scene cannot reasonably treat these omissions as errors. If we disregard them, Cambridge's $6\frac{1}{2}$ lines contain only 1 omission and 1 substitution; all of his cues are word perfect. (By contrast, Scroop in 12 lines has 5 substitutions, 2 interpolations, 1 omission, and errors in 2 out of 6 cues; Grey in $4\frac{1}{2}$ lines has 3 substitutions, 1 omission, 1 interpolation, and errors in 1 of 3 cues.) It seems reasonably clear then that Gower doubled Cambridge. This is probably the only doubling he did which involved speaking parts,[1] but he must have been present in 2.4 as a mute French lord, and in 1.2, either as one of Henry's 'Attendants', or as the mute Bishop of Ely. He almost certainly did not double the mute second French ambassador, for the speeches immediately after the entrance of the ambassadors are probably the most poorly reported in the scene.

Exeter, who, unless he doubled the Governor of Harfleur, did no doubling at all, requires more extended discussion. His $105\frac{1}{2}$ lines[2] contain the following errors:

substitutions	49
omitted words	1
omitted phrases	8 (+ 3?)
minor transpositions	0
major transpositions	1?
interpolations	2?
paraphrase	1
misattributions	4?

The rate of substitution is only marginally higher than Gower's; the rate of omissions, interpolations, and transpositions is markedly lower, perhaps as a consequence of Exeter's speaking verse. But in striking contrast to this over-all accuracy, Exeter's part appears to contain a number of major and serious errors, which presumably

[1] He *could* have doubled Salisbury or York in 4.3, but need not have done, and the quality of the reporting does not inspire confidence.

[2] Again, as in the figures for Gower, I have discounted any lines which might be regarded as deliberate Q omissions.

account for the hesitation sometimes expressed about his participation in the reconstruction.

Four of these errors are apparent misattributions in Exeter's own part. The first, Q's assignment to Exeter of Westmoreland's line 'Shall we call in th' Ambassador, my Liege?' (148) is probably the consequence of two features of the adaptation—its omission of the two preceding lines (rendered superfluous by the omission of 1.1, and the entrance of the Bishops with the court) and its omission of 262–82 (containing, with much else, Westmoreland's only other speech in the scene). With Westmoreland thus effectively abolished as a dramatic presence, to give him the first speech of the play (and nothing else) would have been inept, and the line might naturally be transferred to Exeter, easily the most important of the English nobles, and the one given pride of place in the original text.

The second misattribution occurs in 2.2, and also involves Westmoreland, who has again clearly been removed from the scene: his one speech disappears, along with Henry's reference to him at 698. The first two lines of the scene create no problems; the second, Exeter's, is word perfect, as is his cue (the last five words of the preceding line). Then follows a cut of five lines, involving two unnecessary speeches. The next speech should have been Exeter's, but, because of the intervening cut, this is now dramatically awkward. If we kept the Folio text, but omitted the five lines omitted by Q, we would have:

> They shall be apprehended by and by.
> Nay, but the man that was his bedfellow,
> Whom he hath dull'd and cloy'd . . .

In F, Exeter says 'Nay' because he is contradicting the preceding speaker; as the preceding speech has in Q been omitted, not only has he nothing left to contradict (Q changes 'Nay' to 'I'), but he is put in the position of contradicting—or agreeing with—himself.[1] The simplest solution to this difficulty would be to give the speech to Exeter's interlocutor—which, according to the Quarto, is exactly what was done. Exeter is then given the following speech, a speech which does not exist in the Folio: 'O the Lord of Masham.'

---

[1] If Q had kept 'Nay', it might have been defended as expressing Exeter's own incredulity, rather than his reaction to someone else. But this, though psychologically possible, seems dramatically awkward, especially when the second Chorus, and the immediately preceding five lines (which would lay the grounds for his incredulity) have been omitted. In any case, the alteration to 'I' suggests that this interpretation was not attempted.

Technically this must be described as an interpolation, but there is no reason to doubt that it was spoken on-stage, and equally no reason to assume that the adaptation-Exeter was himself originally responsible for it. Dramatically the addition has the merit of identifying the 'bedfellow' of the preceding speech, and thereby concentrating the audience's attention on Scroop, and providing a focal relationship in the following dialogue.[1]

The third misattribution is combined with Exeter's single major transposition. Exeter's last words in the Folio text of 2.4 are

> Dispatch vs with all speed, least that our King
> Come here himselfe to question our delay;
> For he is footed in this Land already.

In Q the first two lines disappear altogether, and the third is transposed to the beginning of the scene and spoken by the French King:

> You see the King of England is not slack,
> For he is footed on this land alreadie.

Apparently, someone—either the adapter, or Exeter himself—has deliberately moved the line. If the reporter moved it, he would have done so in order to provide some coherent dialogue for a part of the scene neither he nor his colleague remembered at all well. As Gower was himself on-stage in 2.4 as a mute French lord, this seems unlikely. If it were the case, however—and the reporters nowhere else behaved in this way—it is difficult to understand why the two preceding lines of Exeter's speech were not kept, and left where they stood, for they are perfectly intelligible and dramatic in themselves. If on the other hand the adapter moved the line, he presumably did so as part of a general effort to compress and heighten the first half of the scene. Forty-five of the sixty-nine lines before Exeter's entrance have disappeared from the Quarto without a trace, in a series of coherent omissions (888-90, 893-901, 904-9, 930-7,

---

[1] It is perhaps worth remarking that in Exeter's speeches and throughout this scene Q omits all reference to 'Scroope', consistently referring to him as 'Masham'. This might be the consequence of censorship, or imply something about where the abridgement was performed. Henry le Scrope, 9th Baron Scrope of Bolton (1534-92), was marshal of the army Elizabeth sent in March 1560 to assist the Scottish Protestants in the siege of Leith, an intermediary in the intrigue against the regent Moray in 1567, Mary Stuart's jailer in 1568-9, and active in suppressing the attempt to rescue Mary at Tutbury; on 23 April 1584 he received the Garter. He had two sons, Thomas, who was Baron from 1592 until his death in 1609, and Henry. Henry was the name of the traitor Scroope, as Q records; F reads 'Thomas'.

940–54, 961–3, 964–5). In addition, the French King's first long speech, with its vague 'Thus comes the English with full power vpon vs', and its dignified circumlocutions ('And more then carefully it vs concernes, To answer Royally in our defences') has been replaced by the urgency of 'he is footed on this land alreadie'. The result is a scene less subtle, less complex, and less poetic, but considerably more dramatic, in a straightforward way.

The same alternatives are raised by another major transposition in this scene, one affecting the cue for Exeter's last speech. In the Folio Exeter asks for his dispatch after the French King says, 'Tomorrow shall you know our mind at full' (1035). In the Quarto that line disappears altogether, and in its place is put a corrupt version of the King's *preceding* speech (1007–9). This could be dismissed as simple memorial error, were it not for a punctuation mark. The Folio reads

> *Exe.* . . . .
> Vnlesse the Dolphin be in presence here;
> To whom expressly I bring greeting to.
>   *King.* For vs, we will consider of this further:
> To morrow shall you beare our full intent
> Back to our Brother of England.
>   *Dolph.* For the Dolphin,
> I stand here for him . . .

The Quarto, by omitting the King's speech, goes immediately from Exeter's allusion to the Dauphin's reply; and that this arrangement, obviously more dramatic, was intended seems clearly indicated by the fact that Q puts a question-mark after 'For the Dolphin'—which could hardly be spoken as a question, if the King's speech intervened. This is one of a number of occasions where Q seems to preserve the interpretative punctuation of an actual performance.[1]

The fourth misattribution occurs in 4.3. The Folio reads,

> *Bedf.* Farwell good *Salisbury*, & good luck go with thee:
> And yet I doe thee wrong, to mind thee of it,
> For thou art fram'd of the firme truth of valour.
>   *Exe.* Farwell kind Lord: fight valiantly to day. (2252–5)

Clearly, this is wrong, and all editors since Steevens have transposed the second and third lines to follow the fourth, thereby making them

---

[1] Compare F's 'Then you are a better then the King.' (1891) with Q's 'O then thou art better then the King?'

a part of Exeter's speech. The Quarto omits the first line, and puts the remainder in their proper order, but gives them not to Exeter, but Clarence (= Bedford). This variant is readily explicable as deriving from the same confusion in foul papers that produced the error in F itself. For the nonsense created by the apparent misplacement of the marginal insertion of the second and third lines could be rectified by two different expedients: by transposing the two lines into Exeter's speech (the preference of modern editors, and presumably Shakespeare's own original intention), or by transposing the fourth, to precede them, and replace Bedford's line. If this were done by means of an arrow—beginning to the left of the second 'Farwell' and ending to the left of the first—and Bedford's first line crossed out, the effect would be to reassign, accidentally or deliberately, the entire speech to Bedford. This reassignment might be a 'correction' of purely scribal origin; on the other hand, it might as easily be Shakespeare's own, for an author in copying out his own first draft may not always exactly recall his own previous intentions, or, even if he does, may decide to abandon them, in favour of a new thought. Alternatively, and perhaps more plausibly, the change in attribution might be the adapter's: if we imagine him transcribing the original prompt-copy, making alterations and omissions as he wrote, he might have written the speech-prefix *Clarence*, then either decided to cut the redundant line, or skipped accidentally from the first to the second 'Farwell', immediately below it.

In conclusion, none of the misattributions seems memorial in origin. This means that the single serious failure of memory in Exeter's part is his one resort to paraphrase. The Folio reads,

> For Gouernment, though high, and low, and lower,
> Put into parts, doth keepe in one consent,
> Congreeing in a full and natural close,
> Like Musicke. (326-9)

The Quarto reads:

> For gouernment though high or lowe, being put into parts,
> Congrueth with a mutual consent like musicke.

What I have here called paraphrase is, more precisely, a conjunction of several types of error of varying degrees of seriousness: the omission of 'and lower' (by haplography, whether scribal, compositorial, or memorial), the interpolation of 'being', the substitution of 'or' for 'and', 'with' for 'in', and 'Congrueth' for 'Congreeing' (the u/e variant perhaps a scribal normalization or a misreading, but the inflexion certainly memorial, a grammatical compensation for the omission of the preceding phrase), and the combined conflation and transposition which turns 'doth keepe in one consent . . . in a full and natural close' into 'with a mutual consent'. Only this last error, in fact, is in itself critical, but in combination with an unusual concentration of minor errors, it witnesses to Exeter's most serious lapse of memory.

We have identified—or rather, confirmed—the presence of two memories, at the foundation of the Quarto text. We can now proceed to an examination of the nature of these two memories, as evidenced by their performance throughout the text; but we are already, on the strength of the identifications above, in a position to lay down an important principle, namely, that the Quarto readings which must be taken most seriously—indeed, very seriously—are those in the speeches of Gower, Exeter, and Cambridge, or (though these are rather less reliable) in the cues to those speeches; that, for the speeches of other characters, the Quarto is most reliable for those scenes, or parts of scenes, where both actors were present (1.2, 2.2, end of 2.4, 3.3, end of 3.6, 4.8), but less reliable for those in which only one participated (beginning of 2.4, end of 3.2, beginning of 3.6, middle of 4.1, 4.3, 4.6, 4.7, 5.1, beginning and end of 5.2). Finally, these gradations of reliability can be further sophisticated by applying to them a psychological principle, obvious in itself, and confirmed by the study of other memorial texts, namely, that the memory is most reliable at the beginning of the reconstruction, and progressively deteriorates, by reason of exhaustion and also (if the reconstruction were made as soon as possible after a performance) because the memory itself decays during the time actually consumed in writing down the earlier portions.[1] This rule, though it should have no relevance to the actors' own parts, does affect their accuracy in recalling the speeches of others. Except for the reporters' own roles, then, the most authoritative portions of Q are 1.2, 2.2, the end of 2.4, and 3.2. Of course, we are still only dealing in probabilities,

---

[1] 'When a sequence of items is being memorized in sequence . . . it is the first items in the sequence which are mastered soonest' (Ian Hunter, *Memory*, rev. edn. (Harmondsworth, 1964), 135). Similarly, Greg calls attention to the apparent excellence of the reporting in the first scene of *Orlando Furioso*, hypothesizing that at the beginning of the play the reporter's mind was clearer, that he wrote with greater care, and that his task was made easier by the predominance of formal set speeches (*Two Elizabethan Stage Abridgements*: The Battle of Alcazar *and* Orlando Furioso (Oxford, 1922), 342). All these arguments have an obvious relevance to *Henry V*.

for Q contains memorial and scribal errors even in the reporters' own speeches, and on occasion corrects F even in scenes where neither reporter was present; errors can only be sorted from corrections by the exercise of an editor's critical intelligence, and that intelligence will no doubt lead him to reject most Q variants as worthless. But the probabilities can tell him where to look most carefully, where to concentrate the exercise of his intelligence, where to pay most heed to the testimony of Q. This is especially true when we can overlay this set of probabilities derived from Q itself with another set of probabilities, derived from F; the establishment of the text will require an editor's most serious attention when there is a juncture of complementary probabilities, the probability of accuracy in certain scenes and speeches of Q combining with the probability of corruption in the Folio pages set by Compositor B. B set all of 2.2; he set Exeter's speeches in 4.6, Gower's in 4.7, and Gower's in the latter part of 5.1.

Such calculations can be made even more exact by an examination of the nature of the two memories involved, and of their working methods, as revealed by an examination of the entire Quarto text.

The first question to be asked in such an investigation is whether the reporters were familiar with the text of the full version of the play. This has been contended by Duthie, on the evidence of a detailed examination of verbal corruption in Q (pp. 119-28), but before turning to a consideration of that evidence, and of Duthie's methodology, two facts of a rather different kind need to be considered. The first is the appearance in Q, at the end of 3.7, of the couplet which stands in F at the end of 4.2 (a scene omitted from Q). This in itself is persuasive evidence that at least one of the reporters was familiar with the full version, for the couplet—'Come, come, away: The Sun is hie, and we weare out the day' (Q)—makes little sense at the end of the French night scene.[1] But an alternative explanation must be considered. The omission of 4.2, and of the Chorus in Act 4, both necessitated by casting difficulties, may in turn have altered retrospectively the nature of 3.7, now the final appearance of the French before the battle. The line and a half from 4.2 may have been tagged on to the end of 3.7 as a consequence, in order to get the French into battle, as it were. The conflation would have been made possible by the omission of the following Chorus, which fixes the time of the preceding scene, and by the excision of

[1] The couplet would have been Exeter's entrance cue for 4.3, in an unabridged text.

several time-references which appear in the Folio text of that scene. But one of these remains—'Will it neuer be morning?' (D2^v, 23)—and its presence can only be explained by the supposition that the reporter remembered, and incorporated in the Quarto text, details omitted from the abridgement. This is, of course, the very hypothesis we were trying to avoid in the first place, and, as some contamination from the earlier text is required, there seems no reason to posit any deliberate effort to conflate the two scenes.

This clear instance of memorial contamination from the unabridged text must be related to a major crux in 4.1. The Quarto, having omitted Henry's soliloquy, would not need Erpingham's entrance and interruption (2136-40) to serve as a bridge into Henry's prayer. In fact, the interruption would become awkward, for Erpingham would need to enter the moment after the soldiers had left. Without Erpingham, Henry could proceed immediately to his prayer, Gloucester entering afterwards to remind him that 'The day, my friends, and all things stay for me.' But instead, the Quarto presents us with one of its most serious puzzles: having dispensed with the need for Erpingham, and all previous mention of Erpingham, it here calls for Erpingham's appearance, but gives him nothing to say, nothing to do, and no opportunity even to be addressed. Moreover, it calls for him in an impossible stage direction. After Henry's speech about clipping crowns, the Quarto reads:

> *Exit the souldiers.*
> *Enter the King, Gloster, Epingham, and*
> *Attendants.*
> K. O God of battels steele my souldiers harts,
>
> (E1, 19-22)

The anomaly of this entrance direction has nothing to do with any aesthetic objections we might have to Henry speaking his prayer in such a public context. It simply does not belong in this place. Whoever wrote '*Exit the souldiers*' clearly intended Henry to remain on the stage, for he deliberately specified that only the soldiers were to exit. Whoever, after Henry's prayer, wrote '*Enter Gloster*' clearly did not intend Gloucester to enter before the prayer began. The group entrance might be dismissed as an inaccurate collective entry, of a kind occasionally found in texts of the period—except that this is the only instance of such an error in the Quarto, and that such errors usually occur in authorial or scribal texts.

It was Duthie (pp. 126–8) who first suggested that the anomalous direction would not be anomalous if it stood at the beginning of this scene. Duthie advances a complicated and unconvincing explanation of how the direction could have been misplaced: the Quarto text was originally a report of a full performance, which included the opening dialogue omitted from the printed text; an adapter had then annotated this report, as the first draft of a prompt-book, and after a transcript was made had sold it, heavily marked, to the printer; the adapter had crossed out all the dialogue at the start of the scene, but inadvertently had not scored the entrance direction, which stood at the head of the sheet; this sheet was misplaced, being interposed between the exit of the soldiers and the beginning of Henry's speech; the compositor faithfully printed it, where it stood. The extreme complexity of this hypothesis, its assumption of the boundless stupidity of a compositor, and its reliance on the unlikely premise of an annotated report (which has been refuted in the preceding chapter), all contribute to its unpersuasiveness. There is in fact a far simpler explanation. That the anomalous stage direction should have stood at the start of the scene, I have no doubt. That the initial Erpingham episode was omitted in the adaptation, I have no doubt. But that the reporter behind the Quarto text was familiar, at some time, with the full version has already been established by his interpolation of the lines from 4.2. The reporter, then, has interpolated an entrance which he remembered from the earlier, fuller version[1] (just as, on other occasions, he interpolated, in the wrong context, phrases from that version). He has interpolated the entrance here because this is the only other time that Erpingham appeared and spoke in the original play; the process of association is self-evident. Nevertheless, the reporter made no attempt to assimilate this memory into his version of the scene. But this accords with his practice elsewhere, and is perfectly natural for a man trying to put down on paper as much as he can remember as quickly as possible. For this reason we find in the Quarto fragments of sentences which clearly derive from the Folio but make nonsense in the text as it stands, for intervening lines or connective phrases have been omitted.

> For once the Eagle, England being in pray,
> To his vnfurnish nest the weazel Scot
> Would suck her egs, playing the mouse in absence of the cat.
>
> (A3ᵛ, 13–15)

[1] For an example of such a 'fossil stage direction' appearing in a bad quarto, see Greg, *Abridgements*, 345.

As a series of psychological experiments has shown, a person trying to remember and retell a story has two sometimes-conflicting aims: comprehensiveness (to remember all he can) and intelligibility (to make sense).[1] When the desire for intelligibility dominates, he will invent what he cannot remember; when the desire for comprehensiveness dominates, he will include lumps of unassimilated but accurate detail. The Quarto text strongly suggests a reporter occasionally willing to sacrifice intelligibility to comprehensiveness. And this is natural, for a person writing a story down (unlike a person retelling it live) feels that he can go back later and smooth the rough edges, though in fact he may never do so—as the reporters of this quarto apparently did not.

We will return in a moment to the reporters' familiarity with the unabridged text, but as the preceding paragraph raises an issue crucial to our evaluation of the Quarto, it seems appropriate to discuss briefly some striking examples of the reporters' working methods. One occurs in 4.4. The Folio reads,

> *Pist.* Owy, cuppele gorge permafoy pesant, vnlesse
> thou giue me Crownes, braue Crownes; or mangled shalt
> thou be by this my Sword.
>
> (2419–21)

This becomes in Q

> *Pist.* Onye ma foy couple la gorge.
> Vnlesse thou giue to me egregious raunsome, dye.
>   One poynt of a foxe.

What has clearly happened is that the original speech in F has been confused with another, earlier speech of Pistol's, omitted by Q:

> . . . thou dyest on point of Fox, except O Signieur
> thou doe giue to me egregious Ransome.
>
> (2394–5)

The similarities of content and wording have caused the reporter to remember the earlier speech, when he wanted the later; and this has in turn reminded him of the phrase 'on point of Fox', which he has evidently written in the margin, without much if any attempt to connect it explicitly with what follows or precedes. A similar explanation presumably underlies two further typographical peculiarities in Q. Both the couplet interpolated from 4.2 to serve as the

---

[1] A convenient description of the Bartlett experiments can be found in Hunter's *Memory*, 143–69.

ending of 3.7 (D3, 34-5), and the final couplet of 4.5 (E3, 32-3) are indented, as though to indicate a change of speaker, but no speaker is indicated. Bibliographical explanations for these anomalies are possible, but it is consistent with much other evidence to suppose that they derive from copy, indicating that the reporters were not sure to whom to assign the line, and so, for the moment, left it unassigned, and never returned to supply the omission.

The above discussion of Q's conflation of two of Pistol's speeches illustrates the procedure Duthie developed for the analysis of memorial corruption, and one which he specifically applied to *Henry V*, in an attempt to establish the reporters' familiarity with passages omitted from Q. While not disputing the correctness of his conclusion—which seems decisively supported by 3.7 and 4.1—nor the accuracy of his description of the mental operations behind certain memorial substitutions, like 'unfurnisht' for 'unguarded' (316), I think the value of his methodology must be tempered by an awareness of its limitations, the most serious being the fact that it can explain *anything*: a word being repeated, a word not being repeated, a word omitted, the same word interpolated, any transposition, the substitution of any word for any other word. It could be used to establish that any one collateral text of a play was in fact a memorial reconstruction of the other. The method is only valuable when the conclusions which it supports are already beyond a reasonable doubt. It is thus of strictly limited value in enabling an editor to sort corruption from correction in the readings of Q.

If the reporter(s) were familiar with 4.2, they must have been familiar with the play in a performance not affected by limitations of casting; as they were clearly familiar with an uncut version of 4.1 as well, and probably (on Duthie's evidence) of 1.1, it seems reasonable to assume that they had come into contact—either as spectators, or actors—with the play as performed by the Chamberlain's Men. This fact might be important in a number of ways. At the very minimum it establishes that 1.1, 4.2, and the beginning of 4.1 were not omitted from normal London performances of the play. It also lends plausibility to Duthie's evidence of possible contamination from the full versions of 3.1 and 3.2. But more important, it is a valuable clue in any investigation of the circumstances of the abridgement itself, and the nature of the reconstruction. As we have already established (pp. 98-9), Q is a report of the abridgement, not a report made in order to construct an abridgement; therefore the adapter must have had access to a text of the full version. Q was constructed by two actors who performed in the abridgement; as their knowledge of the full text can only have derived from witnessing or participating in a performance of it, it would be simplest to assume that their knowledge of both versions derives from the same cause, professional participation, probably of the same roles. But though this is the simplest reconstruction of the antecedents of Q, it is by no means the only one, for a good text of the unabridged version might have been procured by borrowing or stealing a privately circulated transcript, and the reporters' familiarity with it might be no more than the consequence of having seen it performed (actors do sometimes observe their colleagues), and even if the reporters had participated in Globe performances, they might have taken different roles in the abridgement (though this seems uneconomical). If they did play the same roles in the full version, there may have been little need to re-copy their parts; any omissions or required alterations might be made on the originals, and this would considerably reduce the number of stages of transmission, for their own parts at least. But in the absence of external evidence, I see little hope of our reducing these competing possibilities to anything approaching certainty, though an answer would in at least a few respects assist our evaluation of the reporters' strengths and weaknesses.

We may begin by noticing the absence from Q of certain types of corruption prominent in other contemporary memorial texts. Outside the passages of paraphrase–pastiche in the French scenes, there are no instances of padding, of non-Shakespearian dialogue constructed to provide necessary links and a coherent text. *Henry V* is the only bad quarto without 'a considerable amount of non-Shakespearean matter' (Hart, p. 78), the bad quarto with the fewest words that do not appear in Shakespeare's vocabulary (Hart, p. 33), and the only bad quarto which shows no evidence of memorial contamination from *other* plays (Hart, p. 391). There appears to be no evidence of the reporter going back over and 'revising' his own work;[1] indeed, there is considerable evidence that such revision, though perhaps intended, never took place. There are none of the expansive, narrative stage directions which characterize most reported texts, and which provide so much valuable evidence of contemporary stage practice; the stage directions are disappointingly

---

[1] Such revision is postulated by Duthie for certain passages of Q1 *Hamlet*; see *The 'Bad' Quarto of* Hamlet (Cambridge, 1941), 116, 172–5.

curt, very much in the style of a prompt-book.[1] Moreover, if the reporters had participated in performances of the full version, it is striking that they made so little use of it, not even attempting to include parts of it with which they must at some point have been familiar. All of this evidence, and a good deal else, conforms to a single hypothesis, that the reporters of this particular bad quarto were unusually conscientious and restrained. To adopt the categories most often applied to agents of transmission: the reporters of this bad quarto, unlike the reporters of some other bad quartos, were naïve, rather than sophisticated. What corruption they perpetrated was passive, and the result of mere deficiency, rather than active, deliberate, or editorial.

These conclusions are confirmed by the remainder of the evidence. The most important variants in this respect are interpolations. Most of these fall into clear and predictable categories: interjections (excluding profanities, which may have been deliberately omitted from F, rather than memorially interpolated in Q), vocatives, repeated cues, unnecessary conjunctions and connectives. Catch-phrases, like Fluellen's 'look you', and other words or phrases which occur repeatedly, provide obvious opportunities for confusion about the number of times to repeat them, and lists or catalogues provide similar scope for confusion as to the number of items. These are all memorial errors of the most trivial kind. So too are interpolations of single words—when it is clear (as it often is not) that the apparent interpolation in Q is not instead the result of an omission in F. Other interpolations are in fact no more than long-range transpositions of material from its proper place to an improper one. To this category of Q variant an editor can safely pay little or no attention, as long as he isolates, for special consideration, the important cases of potential censorship and compositorial omission in F itself.

There remain, however, two categories of interpolation which, though their numbers are small, require more extended comment. First among these are interpolations like those in the passages of French dialogue (3.4, 4.4). These passages are the only ones in the play clearly given over to paraphrase, based upon a knowledge of their basic content retranslated back into French, or the appearance

---

[1] I do not mean to imply that the reporters had access to a prompt-book; but they would be professionally familiar with them, and their decisions about what stage directions to include, and how to phrase them, might naturally be influenced by such experience.

of French ('remembre', 'rehersera', 'recontera'); nor is it difficult to understand why they should differ from the rest of the text in this way. Interpolation, as a specific phenomenon, is in these scenes simply a symptom of the graver disease of paraphrase. This is also true of a number of other interpolations which, like that from 1.2 discussed above (p. 140), are the consequence of contextual para-phrase.[1] The concentration of this kind of interpolation–paraphrase in scenes otherwise poorly reported, and in which the presumed reporters themselves took no part, is self-evident, as is the fact that an editor need pay no attention whatever to these Quarto readings.

The second category of interpolation is more important, in that it appears to involve theatrical additions which post-date the foul papers behind F. Several of these have already been mentioned, and as the number of cases remaining is quite small, they can be discussed individually.

Four involve Pistol; specifically, Pistol's exits. At the end of 2.3 Pistol admonishes someone with the words 'Keepe faste thy buggle boe'. As his three preceding speeches are directed to (or about) the Hostess, it would be natural to suppose that he is again addressing her here. *Buggle-boo*, a Scots word for 'goblin', first appears in England in 1598, in William Lisle's translation of Du Bartas: 'Another in his moodes / Is like a Bugger-bo [1625 Buggle-bo] and strayes amids the woodes.'[2] The *Dictionary of National Biography* records that Lisle was a scholar, born in Somerset, who lived most

---

[1] Other examples are: (1) 'No [fur, no fur]' (D5ᵛ, 5), replacing an entire speech (826–9); (2) '[Well sir *Iohn* is gone. God be with him]' (D4ᵛ, 6), transposing the announcement of Falstaff's death out of the preceding speech, and then paraphrasing 'Would I were with him, wheresomere hee is, eyther in Heauen, or in Hell' (830–1), in the process reversing its emphases, so that Quickly must reply 'I' instead of 'Nay'; (3) '[You see the King of England is not slacke]' (C1, 23), discussed above (p. 138); (4) '[Before God here is hote service]' (C2ᵛ, 9), a paraphrase of 'the knocks are too hot ... the humor of it is too hot' (1121–3); (5) '[*Nim*. Tis honor, and there's the humor of it]' (C2ᵛ, 12), a paraphrase and misattribution of the cue required for the Boy's following speech ('I'd giue all my honor' Q; 'I would giue all my fame' F), a cue originally provided by Pistol's mention of 'immortal Fame' (1128, omitted from Q); (6) '[I would not stay]' (C2ᵛ, 16), a paraphrase of 'my purpose should not fayle with me' (1131), his purpose being flight; (7) '[Well I would I were once from them ... Well, if they will not leaue me]' (C2ᵛ, 22, 30), a repeated paraphrase of the general drift of the Boy's speech, which, like the whole of this scene, is very poorly reported; (8) 'Now [at this instant]' (E1ᵛ, 26), a transposed substitution for the omitted 'today' (2261); (9) the last five lines of the play, a miserable paraphrase of the end of the wooing scene, which is itself miserably reported throughout.

[2] *The Colonies of Bartas* ... (1598), K1ʳ; para. 59. A revised version of this work forms part of Lisle's *Part of Du Bartas* ... (1625). I am indebted to Professor George Walton Williams for pointing out to me the meaning of Q's line.

of his life in Cambridgeshire; by 1598 then, the Scots word had entered the mainstream of English usage. Moreover, Lisle's identification of the word with a spirit that 'strayes' (1625 'straies ev'er') helps to define its significance in Q1: Pistol, who in F admonishes his wife to 'keepe close, I thee command' (a line omitted by Q), doubting Quickly's fidelity in his absence, is telling her to 'restrain her wandering spirit'. Q's line is thus less an interpolation than a substitute for F's 'keepe close, I thee command'. The particularity, even eccentricity, of this substitution makes it difficult to attribute to the reporter; but it does not seem to me particularly Shakespearian or exceptionally apt, and I am therefore inclined to refer it to an actor.

The second interpolation, in 3.6, is more acute. Pistol is given another line before his exit, and Fluellen a reply.

> *Pist.* I say the fig within thy bowels and thy durty maw.
> *Exit Pistoll.*
> *Fle.* Captain *Gour*, cannot you hear it lighten & thunder?

In this case, of course, Pistol's own contribution is less important than the response it elicits, which is not only entirely in character, but wonderfully apt, and among the most effective of the many deflations Pistol is made to suffer.

The third interpolation, in 4.1, is simply a repetition before Pistol's exit of 'My name is Pistol call'd', an unimportant and probably unauthorized line, though it does indicate that Pistol, in 1600, did not hear Henry's 'It sorts well with thy fierceness'. But the most famous of Q's interpolations is the fourth one involving Pistol, when, at the end of 4.6, he is given the last word, 'Couple gorge'. Naturally editors dismiss this as a classic instance of an actor's interpolation, the clown foisting into the text debile jokes of his own devising. But I suspect that, if the line were given a chance in the theatre, it could prove not only funny, but powerful and even, in Pistol's absurd way, moving. After all, in capturing Le Fer Pistol stands on the brink of wealth: in killing him, he kills two hundred crowns, thereby at play's end returning to England poorer and more destitute than ever. This is, so to speak, Pistol's moment of choice, and his moment of greatness: first reacting to the King's command with a look of fiscal outrage, hesitating, eyeing Le Fer, pausing, and then with a shrug returning to the bravado of 'Couple gorge' as he cuts the man's throat. Critics remark on the genius with which great dramatists enact their images, take them literally, transpose them out of imagination into the realm of the shockingly palpable: so, after the comic and unreal hyperbole of Nym's and MacMorris's and Pistol's talk of throat-cutting, it is Pistol, the high priest of literary *grand guignol*, who actually and before our eyes cuts a man's throat. This could be a moment at once endearing, pathetic, and terrible, when an audience chokes on its own laughter, and scenes 4 and 5 may have been transposed solely for the sake of this line. The 1966 Royal Shakespeare Company production retained the line, which provides an individual and thereby inescapable focus for the abstract 'Let every soldier kill his prisoners'; Pistol spoke it as he coldly murdered the one French prisoner on-stage, struggling and held captive by a straining English soldier, a moment of brutality remembered and remarked upon by several critics. (Its other nuances the RSC squandered by repeatedly pronouncing it 'Coopey la Georgie'[1] and by postponing Le Fer's scene until *after* scene 6.)

The fact that these four interpolations all involve one character, that the actor is the play's clown, and that each affects an exit—a moment dearer to the hearts of actors than anything but an entrance—may combine to convince some critics that all are 'actor's interpolations'. (As Shakespeare was himself an actor, this expression, so beloved of textual criticism, might be accused of ambiguity; but since the ambiguity is useful, I will let it stand.) This is probably true of the third, which involves a simple and unmeaning repetition. 'Keep faste thy buggle boe' might also be explained as an ad lib, particularly if an actor had ever heard the picturesque phrase used by a husband to his wife; 'Couple gorge' could be explained as the clown's infamous inability to resist repeating a gag. But these explanations are as conjectural and subjective as the supposition that Shakespeare himself added the lines. Moreover, they are, in the final analysis, irrelevant, in that the origin of these interpolations need not affect their *authority*. Pistol, in rehearsal one morning, filling up a place in the English army in 4.6, may have asked, 'Wouldn't it be better if we *used* Pistol in this scene?' or 'Wouldn't it be in character if . . .'; or he may actually have just said 'Couple gorge', in a rehearsal or a performance. What matters, from the perspective of textual authority, is whether Shakespeare approved of the idea, even if it were not his own. Theatre is a collaborative enterprise, and Shakespeare was collaborating with the best actors

[1] Gareth Lloyd Evans, *Stratford-upon-Avon Herald*, 19 August 1966. For details and reviews of the 1966 production I have consulted the prompt-book and the collection of Theatre Records, both at the Shakespeare Centre Library, Stratford.

of his time; he was an actor himself, and hardly likely to despise the opinion of fellow professionals; and unlike some dramatists then and now, he shows no signs of having regarded his work as 'literature', above and beyond the grimy realm of entertainment. Consequently, if the objective of textual criticism is to recover, as far as possible, an author's fair copy of his own work, it must not be supposed that this ideal fair copy will in all cases antedate rehearsal and performance, of the criticism of the author's colleagues and friends.[1]

The final criteria for acceptance or rejection of such passages must be, can only be, critical and aesthetic. The fact that these passages occur in a bad quarto is—in this instance, at least—hardly relevant, for there can be little question of the reporter inventing these lines. Consequently, as here the reporter seems certainly to be describing what he did hear and did see, the choice for an editor is between the reading of foul papers (antedating the ideal fair copy) and the evidence of a theatrical document (postdating the fair copy). These are alternatives an editor encounters often enough elsewhere: not only with the quarto and Folio texts of *2 Henry VI*, *3 Henry VI*, *Richard III*, *Romeo and Juliet*, and *The Merry Wives of Windsor*, but with the good quarto and not-so-good Folio texts of *Love's Labour's Lost*, *A Midsummer Night's Dream*, *The Merchant of Venice*, *Much Ado About Nothing*, *Richard II*, *1 Henry IV*, and *Hamlet* (not to mention *King Lear*). An editor has only his intelligence to guide him.

The concentration on Pistol, however, materially distorts the problem, which involves other actors as well. I have already mentioned theatrical alterations affecting Exeter, Gower, and the Dauphin (one each); Fluellen and Nym are also involved. To begin with, the interpolation in 3.6, if it did originate with an actor, is likelier to have come from Fluellen than Pistol. But there is an unequivocal instance in 3.2. Critics have sometimes remarked on the Folio's slightly unsatisfactory introduction of Fluellen: the spectacle of his beating the Eastcheap regiment up to the breach would be more effective and more meaningful if we knew *who* was doing the beating. The Folio gives no clue to his identity until afterwards; there is no hint, even, of his Welshness. In the theatre, of course, he

---

[1] For a modern example of the editorial difficulties created by a playwright's collaboration with his cast, see Philip Gaskell's *From Writer to Reader* (Oxford, 1978), 245–62. The relative literary status of Shakespeare and Stoppard is irrelevant to the editorial problem.

is Welsh the moment he opens his mouth, but the Quarto goes further than this, suggesting, in his first speech, not only his nationality but his comic stature as well. It does this simply by turning 'Vp to the breach' into 'Vp to the breaches', and then repeating the malapropriate injunction ('You rascals, will you not vp to the breaches?'). It is hard to imagine a more economical and effective expedient for guiding the audience's first reactions.

The Quarto additions involving Nym, both in 2.1, are more complicated. The simpler of the two, 'I shall have my eight shillings I wonne of you at beating?' (604 + 1), has been accepted by most editors, on the assumption that the Folio inadvertently omitted it. But the Folio makes perfect sense without the line: Bardolph threatens to kill the man who makes the first thrust, Pistol acquiesces, Nym remains sulkily intransigent, Bardolph threatens him specifically, and then Pistol magnanimously offers his noble. There is no *need* for the Quarto line; though it does make the action more explicit, in doing so it marginally alters our impression of the two combatants. Thus, though an editor could certainly defend his acceptance of the line, it would not necessarily be wise to do so on the assumption of a simple Folio omission; nor would it be wise to repose any simple faith in the accuracy of Q's wording. The Quarto here repeats verbatim its version of 594 (F: 'You'l pay me the eight shillings I won of you / at Betting?'), and editors, by adopting F's reading for 594, and Q's for 604 + 1, have almost certainly distorted the intentions of the actor or author responsible for Q's line. The verbatim repetition in Q can be interpreted in either of two ways. If the repetition is intentional, then the reporter has remembered the obvious formal identity of the two speeches, but has slightly botched their actual verbal content—in which case, an editor must take Q as his authority for the existence of the line, but base its exact wording on Folio 594. But if, on the other hand, the repetition is the consequence of memorial contamination—neither reporter was present in this scene—then an editor must attempt to reconstruct the original inferentially. This may seem impossible, but actually it is not, for the simplest solution would be to omit the last six words, so that Nym says only 'I shall have my eight shillings?' This conjecture, which has in fact been adopted in the theatre,[1] is characteristically

---

[1] *The Royal Shakespeare Company's Centenary Production of* Henry V, ed. Sally Beauman (Oxford, 1976), p. 124. I have not found this emendation in any other prompt-book. That Q's line is not strictly necessary can be inferred from the fact that neither Bell's acting edition, Kemble's prompt-book, nor Olivier's film included it.

curt, involves the supposition of an easy memorial error, removes the redundant half of the utterance, and explains the substitution of 'my' for 'the' ('my' being unnecessary with the subordinate clause, but useful in its absence). Either of these reconstructions would be preferable to the present practice.

The Quarto's second addition to this scene is related to its reattribution of 'How now mine Hoaste *Pistoll?*' (532) from Bardolph to Nym. This apparent reattribution has been regarded as no more than the result of the omission of a speech-prefix by the Folio compositor. That this explanation will not serve is suggested by the fact that Q, having given to Nym Bardolph's greeting to Pistol, gives Bardolph *another*, and different, greeting.

> *Enter* Pistoll *and Hostes Quickly, his wife.*
> *Bar.* Godmorrow ancient *Pistoll.*
> Here comes ancient *Pistoll,* I prithee *Nim* be quiet.
> *Nim.* How do you my Hoste?

It is difficult not to relate the interpolated salutation to the subsequent reattribution, and the combined result is a marginally different version of the scene. In F, Bardolph sees Pistol coming, urges Nym to be patient, then addresses Pistol, who takes unexpected offence at his words. In Q, Bardolph sees Pistol coming, shouts a greeting to him and then, while Pistol approaches, urges Nym to be patient; Nym, however, immediately greets Pistol in a provocative manner, and Pistol predictably takes offence. Editors might disagree on the relative merits of these alternatives, as they might disagree on the merits of any variant readings, but the presence of two coherent alternatives seems difficult to deny. However, the editorial task is complicated by disagreement over the insult in 'host', and by a crux later in the scene, over exactly what prompts Quickly's expectation of 'wilful adultery and murder'. In F, she exclaims 'O welliday Lady, if he be not hewne now'; in Q, 'O Lord heeres Corporall *Nims*'. Q's line would make excellent sense in F, where Nym has not yet spoken and has not yet been addressed; F's line would make excellent sense in Q; neither seems particularly apposite to the text in which it occurs. F's reading can be explained or emended; Q's reading can be regarded as a memorial paraphrase of Quickly's surprise. But this latter crux will necessarily affect an editor's attitude to the related issue of Pistol's alternative entrances.

Each of these passages will have to be judged by editors on its own merits, but if rejected the Quarto alternatives must, at the least, be recorded in the collations, and preferably discussed. The sparsity and quality of these variants make such attention possible, but they also, and as importantly, testify to the over-all restraint of the reporters. For the greater the numbers of such variants and the more indifferent their consequences, the more one begins to suspect mere vamping, editorial interference, memorial rewriting, or, at the very least, wholesale 'actors' interpolations'.

If we disregard their relevance to investigations of casting, omissions are in general a less valuable species of error than interpolation in characterizing bad quartos, except insofar as the quantity of omission clearly due to failure of memory tells us something about the mental capacity of the reporters. But in dealing with what is clearly an abridged text, it is impossible to be sure how much omission is deliberate, and how much accidental; one can only distinguish, instead, between rational and nonsensical omissions. Omissions which produce nonsense are fairly certainly memorial;[1] rational omissions, though, may be accidentally rational, or rational because deliberate, or rational because non-sensical omissions have been subsequently repaired by deliberate rewriting. In this quarto there is no evidence of the third, rational-ized species of omission, and a great deal in the general character of the text to argue against it. Beyond this, we can only operate on the basis of two probabilities: that reason is likelier than chance to produce coherence, and that chance is likelier in certain portions of the text than in others. Sometimes—as with the Quarto's omission of the first two lines of 1.2, or of the mention of Westmoreland in 2.2—the absence of passages is clearly the mechanical consequence of abridgements related to casting; elsewhere—as with the omission of the lines in 2.1 blaming Falstaff's death on Henry's treatment of him, or those in 1.2 where Canterbury offers his ecclesiastical bribe—the variants are so in harmony with simplifications evident throughout the text that one has difficulty believing they are anything but deliberate adaptations. But even when such passages are set aside, there remain a good many others where, though deliberation appears probable, one cannot rule out the operation of chance, nor decide *whose* deliberation was responsible.

Of course, no editor will omit any of the passages omitted by Q. But the omissions are nevertheless interesting, for two reasons.

---

[1] Greg points out that in *Orlando Furioso* 'in no single instance has an actual cut proved by the parallel texts produced a grammatical dislocation' (299). Hart comes to similar conclusions from an examination of the *Edmund Ironside* manuscript (126).

First, and most obviously, as documents of the play's theatrical history: many of these omissions occur also in post-Restoration productions. More important, some at least of these omissions may derive from Shakespeare himself. Posterity has a natural interest in preserving every word the national genius wrote, but the genius himself was engaged in the shaping of works of art, and omission is, for any artist, a shaping instrument. Sculpture is, *par excellence*, the art of omission, but all form is a product of decisions about inclusion and exclusion, and whether these decisions are made before of after first putting pen to paper is a mechanical distinction of no real significance to the artistic enterprise itself, however important it may be to textual criticism, or to those interested in the process of creation. In this case we simply have no way of knowing the extent of Shakespeare's responsibility or acquiescence. Some of the Quarto's omissions seem to me not only theatrically expedient, but genuine improvements of the play, of potential interest to anyone interested in literature, and consequently any scholarly edition of the play should give them at least the benefit of an appendix.

As we have already seen, a number of Q changes in speech-ascription are the consequence of casting or related abridgement; several others clearly result from mechanical error, probably in the printing house.[1] Of the remainder, nine, which are almost certainly errors, occur in scenes involving the Eastcheap characters or the French (2.3, 3.2, 3.5, 3.7). There are only six other ascription variants in the remainder of the play, and many of these cannot be simply dismissed as errors: one (532, from Bardolph to Nym) has been accepted by most editors, another (313, from Ely to 'Lord') can be convincingly defended on dramatic grounds; a third (707) involves no more than giving a short speech to one of two characters, rather than both, a change that could be the result of a simple omission at any stage of transmission, or represent a deliberate decision by the two actors involved, or by the adapter—especially as the speech is given to Scroop, much the more important of the two; a fourth (2255, from Exeter to Clarence), already discussed above (pp. 139-40), almost certainly represents the adapted text as performed. This leaves only two cases, both from 4.1. One of these (2056, from Williams to Henry) is clearly wrong, and based upon a kind of transposition: in this passage the two characters

---

[1] The clearest example is the omission of a speech prefix *King* at 2799, so that the list of French dead is read by Exeter. The fact that Q gives Exeter the next speech makes clear that the omission is due to printing house, and not memorial, error.

exchange gloves, repeating the same threats and promises with slight variations of phrasing, and some confusion about who says what first is understandable. The second (2034, from Williams to Bates) is more important, for it not only resolves an obvious dramatic difficulty in F, but seems supported by several modifications to the dialogue itself. F reads:

> *Will.* 'Tis certaine, euery man that dyes ill, the ill vpon
> his owne head, the King is not to answer it.
> *Bates.* I doe not desire hee should answer for me, and
> yet I determine to fight lustily for him.
>
> (2034–7)

Q reads:

> *3. Lord.* Yfaith he saies true:
> Euery mans fault on his owne head,
> I would not haue the king answere for me
> Yet I intend to fight lustily for him.

The third soldier in Q is the Folio Bates; Williams is always identified as the second. ('Lord' is a printing error, affecting all the soldiers' speeches on this page.[1]) Clearly, the dialogue in Q is poorly reported, but it is at least worth remarking that Q does omit the one phrase which by its repetition signals a change of speaker, and in doing so alters the consequently ambiguous 'hee' to 'the king'. Moreover, the reporter, though he may have faltered about the wording, clearly remembered the gist of its content, and if he remembered so much, it is difficult to believe he could in this case have forgotten who said it, for who says it is the more important and more striking dramatic fact: someone is acquiescing in Henry's reasoning, either his accuser, Williams (in which case the volte-face cannot fail to impress us), or Bates (in which case the silence of Williams cannot but be conspicuous—especially considering what follows). Finally, this variant is, in the context of Q, strikingly anomalous, being the only respect in which Q complicates, rather than simplifies, the portrayal of Henry and the moral issue. All this evidence, particularly in combination, strongly suggests that Q represents a deliberate, pre-adaptation revision, a conclusion which has much to recommend it on aesthetic grounds, as well.

Q's stage directions, long considered inexplicable, are for the most part vindicated by an understanding of the exigencies of its

---

[1] For an explanation of the error, see T. L. Berger, 'The Printing of *Henry V*, Q1', *The Library*, VI, 1 (1979), 114–25. I had arrived at similar conclusions independently.

casting. As a consequence, the standard of accuracy of its stage directions now appears quite high, and this will affect the weight we give its testimony in two troubling directions from Act 3.

Half-way through 3.2, Q and F read *Enter Gower* (1171), which editors emend to *Enter Gower and Fluellen*. Fluellen entered at line 1136, but he clearly left the stage at 1144, beating Pistol, Bardolph, and Nym off the stage. The Boy remains for a soliloquy, so that Fluellen must be off-stage for some time. The text must therefore be emended. But if editors accept the emendation *Enter Gower and Fluellen*, they should also mark a new scene. The stage has been cleared, time may have passed, the place may have changed. In the Olivier film, this change of scene was explicit; in modern productions it is often unmistakably implied. Whether any passage of time is implied makes considerable difference in our impressions of the difficulty and duration of the Harfleur campaign.

But how do we account for the agreement of Q and F? Cairncross's explanation, contamination of F by Q, has been discredited. Q and F must therefore have made the error independently, and it is possible to see why they have done so. As explanation for the error in F, three possibilities suggest themselves. Fluellen might not appear until after Gower calls him ('Captain Fluellen . . .'), in which case the entry might have been omitted by Shakespeare, leaving it to be inferred. Or, the Boy's soliloquy might be a later addition to the manuscript, so that Gower would originally have entered just after Fluellen drove the others off the stage—in which case Shakespeare simply forgot to alter the stage direction when he inserted the Boy's speech. Or, the omission of Fluellen's name is simply one of a number of instances where re-entrances after a brief interval cause textual problems, because of the omission of either the exit or the re-entry.

As for the Quarto text, though wrong, it is logical. We seem to be dealing with a relatively simple case of memorial foreshortening, the mind of the reporter summarizing the scene along these lines: 'It starts off with the Eastcheap characters, then afterwards Fluellen beats them off-stage, and the rest of the scene is between him and Gower.' As summary, this is accurate, but one easily sees how it could lead to inaccuracies of detail. But there is also, I think, another and perhaps more pertinent explanation; for Gower himself was certainly one of the reporters behind Q, and if Fluellen had entered with him, he could hardly fail to remember the fact, foreshortening or no. The sequence of events must therefore have been somewhat as follows: Fluellen entered from one door of the stage, and left it by another, beating the laggards up to the breach; after the Boy's soliloquy, Gower then entered from the first door, searching for Fluellen, who would in turn naturally re-enter from the second. This means that, in terms of an actor's written part, or his experiences of the performance (waiting just off-stage for his cue to enter), there might be no sense of entering *with* Fluellen: they enter from different doors, perhaps invisible to one another, and may not even enter quite simultaneously.[1] Moreover, if Gower had been waiting near the first door for any length of time before his own cue, the mental foreshortening of the scene would be even more probable, for Gower would have seen Fluellen go out of that door, and then in a few moments he himself would go out of it, with Fluellen already on, or just returning to, the stage.

In this case Q and F independently agree in error. This appears to occur again in the next scene, where Henry delivers an ultimatum, forty-three lines long, to Harfleur. In reply, the Governor surrenders the garrison. In both Q and F *Enter the Governor* does not occur until after Henry finishes speaking, but editors almost always give the Governor's entrance, above, at the start of the scene (the more usual procedure for staging sieges). Recent editors, troubled by the agreement of Q and F, have followed J. H. Walter in having the Governor enter initially above, then descend to the main stage after Henry's speech. But Henry, in reply to his capitulation, says 'Open your gates', which would be ludicrous had the gates already been opened to allow the Governor on to the main stage. Likewise, A. R. Humphreys (New Penguin) leaves the Governor's entry where Q and F put it, but invents some anonymous citizenry to man the walls as Henry speaks. To give the Governor attendants when he enters might be an unexceptionable editorial licence—but attendants forty-three lines *before* he enters? And though the attendants might not have been mentioned in foul papers, why should they be absent from a text based on actual performance? Why, in particular, should this fact have been overlooked in an excellently reported scene, where *both* reporters were present? The agreement of Q and F cannot be due to contamination. Even if Cairncross's theory of annotated quarto copy were correct, Compositor A must have

---

[1] Exactly the same error occurs at the beginning of 3.6, and must be due to the same cause. Q has '*Enter Gower*', F '*Enter Captaines, English and Welch, Gower and Fluellen*'. As Gower's first words are addressed to Fluellen, F's stage direction must be right, but as Fluellen is coming from the bridge, the two characters must have entered from different directions.

completely reset the opening stage direction for this scene; therefore, if Shakespeare's manuscript contained an earlier entry for the Governor (or citizens), it should have been printed.

Both texts, I think, preserve Shakespeare's intention, an intention less conventional and more dramatic than the emendation. Rather than concentrate our attention upon a minor character who must be silent for forty-three lines, Shakespeare focuses entirely upon Henry and the terror of his ultimatum, part of the scene's tension deriving from the very *absence* of the Governor, the uncertainty whether anyone is listening at all, or (if they are listening) whether Henry's threats are having the least effect. In surviving prompt-books, virtually without exception, if the Governor is brought on-stage early, Henry's speech is severely cut;[1] indeed, with the Governor on-stage, it is unforgivably long. But the 1975 Royal Shakespeare Company production did not shorten the speech. Henry faced the audience to demand Harfleur's surrender, and afterwards the unseen Governor capitulated from the upper circle. Of course, Burbage probably would not have faced the audience, but turned his back to it, far downstage, shouting to his imaginary listeners behind the upstage wall—though, in a non-illusionist theatre, Burbage might well have delivered this set piece to the audience, then wheeled to face upstage, stepping back into the frame as it were, just as the Governor enters to reply. But either arrangement permits a full-throated, frightening volume, which the speech patently requires, a vocal force unimaginable when Henry stands, as he so often does, under the feet of the Governor. The Quarto, the Folio, and the 1975 staging all allow an audience to experience the strain and magnitude of voices across a gulf. For the city of Harfleur, Shakespeare gives us only a wall and the empty space between armies—but only the wall, and the empty space, and Henry's isolation in that space, matter. Henry here as elsewhere speaks most characteristically to an audience without a face: to the absent Dauphin, to Scroop (who exists only insofar as Henry creates him), to his as-yet-unindividuated troops ('Once more unto the breach'), to Montjoy's absent masters, to God, to idol Ceremony, to the invisible populace of Harfleur.

---

[1] With the exception of the 1975 RSC production, none of the prompt-books collated by Nancarrow ('A Stage History of William Shakespeare's *King Henry the Fifth*', unpublished doctoral dissertation, Birmingham, 1975) or in the Shakespeare Centre Library collection gives this speech in full. I say 'virtually' without exception simply as a caution. Q's own omissions from the speech are, as I suggested above (pp. 129-30), a natural consequence of thoroughgoing abridgement.

The important additions, omissions, speech ascriptions and stage direction variants in Q, because few in number, can be discussed individually in some detail, but for the last two categories of editorially significant error—transposition and substitution—involving as they do legions of variants, we can do no more than describe the perimeters of the problem.

Most of the transpositions have no authority at all, for transposition is among the easiest forms of memorial error. Nevertheless, transpositions come in a variety of types and sizes, and a brief analysis of these may enable us to isolate cases of potential editorial significance.

1. Transposition of words or phrases in doublets ('hardiness and policy') or catalogues.

2. Transposition of words performing the same syntactical function in grammatically parallel phrases ('Like Turkish mute, shall haue a tonguelesse mouth' F, 379; 'like toonglesse mutes' Q).

3. Transposition of vocatives, interjections, and other floating elements (thus, therefore, etc.) within a sentence.

4. Transposition as an element in a larger dislocation or paraphrase.

5. Those memorial substitutions which are in fact transpositions of words or phrases out of their proper context into another.

6. Transpositions of clauses or sentences within a speech.

7. Transposition of whole speeches.

8. Transposition of parts of speeches (clauses, whole sentences) into other speeches (= conflation).

9. Transposition of scenes.

Few of these transpositions can be of any authority, for the errors involved are ones compositors are extremely unlikely to make, and consequently there is little reason to suspect that the variants might be due to error in F and accuracy in Q. However, some limited allowance must be made for ambiguities of placement resulting from marginal insertions in foul papers (2253-4), and for deliberate revision, by the author or an adapter (the transposition of 4.4 and 4.5).

10. Transposition of words immediately juxtaposed, especially subject-verb, or subject-object.

Because such transposition, in contrast to the others, may be made by compositors easily enough, an editor must always consider the possibility of error in F, especially when F preserves the more

commonplace and/or the less metrical of the two possible construc-
tions. Thus, editors almost always emend Pistol's 'I defie thee againe'
(F, 573) to 'I thee defie agen' (Q). But there are other examples
which involve precisely the same principles: for instance, 'Fiue hundred poore I haue in yeerely pay' (F, 2150; 'haue I' Q) and 'For that
I haue layd by my Maiestie' (F, 426; 'haue I' Q). Certainly, editors
must at least record such variants, and a good many may prefer Q.

If transpositions are legion, substitutions are ubiquitous; nor do
they yield so easily to editorial categories. Most involve unmistakable debasement, or memorial contamination from another context
(Transposition 5), or indifferent synonyms, which an editor can
and should reject from his collations as well as his text. But an editor
cannot ignore substitutions altogether, both because the Folio
compositors were themselves capable of substitution and debasement, and because the foul papers behind F may not have included
Shakespeare's final verbal revisions. An editor must therefore
initially consider every Q variant, and on the relatively infrequent
occasions when Q offers either a more unusual or (in his judgement)
a clearly superior reading, he would be obliged to record it, and
entitled to adopt it. The number of such readings adopted from Q
will necessarily remain relatively small, and in isolating them an
editor will be guided both by his knowledge of the relative reliability
of different portions of Q and by his analysis of the types and
frequencies of error in the work of the Folio compositors.[1]

The weeding of corruption from authority in the quarto of
Henry V is thus, finally, bound up in the larger study of corruption
and authority throughout the Folio, a study inseparable from the
identification and analysis of the Folio compositors. This larger
investigation is of course relevant to much besides *Henry V*, but that
it will prove most important for the plays which exist in bad
quartos—*Henry V, 2 Henry VI, 3 Henry VI, Richard III, The Merry
Wives of Windsor*—I do not doubt, for it is in precisely these cases
that a text of real but imperfect authority can be juxtaposed with the
known probability of unidentified error in a good text. Thus, the
decisive (over)simplification which divided good quartos from bad,
the twentieth century's first great contribution to the study of
Shakespeare's text, may eventually be modified and corrected by the
twentieth century's second great contribution, the analysis of the
printing of F1.

[1] For an example, see my 'Shakespeare's Leno: *Henry V* IV.v.14', *N & Q*, 224
(1979), pp. 117–18.

POSTSCRIPT: IMPLICATIONS

I HAVE deliberately avoided drawing many parallels between *Henry V* and other texts. The circumstances of *Henry V* may well be unique; I have not yet examined the other bad quartos systematically enough to venture any hypotheses concerning their individual character. But I would claim, with some confidence, that we can have no confidence in the orthodox view of those bad quartos until each has been similarly investigated.

The methodology for such investigations is in principle simple, however complex its applications. We want to determine the relative authority of different portions of both the good and bad texts. For the bad text, this involves three operations: (1) discounting—insofar as possible—corruption introduced by the printer and the scribal intermediaries between authorial papers and the actors' parts, (2) isolating any adaptations which seem due to mechanical theatrical restraints, and (3) identifying and then characterizing the reporter(s). It may well be that for other bad quartos limitations of cast are less significant, but the possibility must always be explored, and the results presented with as much intellectual rigour and detailed attention to evidence as would be expected in an examination of presswork. Moreover, if the theory of memorial reconstruction by an actor or actors is valid, it should *always* be possible to identify the reporter(s). It may not be easy, but it should be possible. Reporter-identification, which has in the past been treated rather impressionistically, in fact requires the same attention to detail, the same rigorous evaluation of evidence, as compositor-identification. For bad quartos at least, identifying the reporter is the more important task.

The resulting map of authority, corruption, and adaptation in the bad text can then be overlaid by a similar map of the good one, constructed by (1) identifying and characterizing the compositors, (2) determining whether the good text has been contaminated by the bad, and (3) identifying the character of its manuscript copy. Juxtaposing these two maps should enable us to isolate far more effectively than in the past verbal corruption and compositorial error in the good text.

But it will also isolate another and equally important class of variants, those for which both texts seem right. Here we confront the spectre of authorial revision. But this should by now be a familiar ghost; it is, in fact, only the spectre of collateral texts. Of course, one of these collateral texts is incomplete and only partially reliable. Nevertheless, given an appropriately thorough investigation of the imperfect text, it should be—and in *Henry V* has been—possible to identify several classes of variant which could represent authorial revision. These are, in an ascending order of certainty:

1. Verbal substitutions, particularly in well-reported portions of the text, which seem superior on critical grounds ('And cryde aloud, tary deare cousin *Suffolke*').

2. Verbal additions which seem 'Shakespearian' ('Captain *Gour*, cannot you hear it lighten & thunder?').

3. Adaptations which are not the result of mechanical imperatives (Clarence for Bedford).

4. Adaptations which run counter to mechanical imperatives (Warwick for Westmoreland, Bourbon for the Dauphin)—particularly if these seem aesthetically superior as well.

As a consequence, editors will now have to make choices where before there seemed no room for choice. Future editors of *Henry V*, for instance, will have to decide whether Bourbon or the Dauphin appears at Agincourt. This makes life more difficult for the editor; but what editor expects life to be easy?